"Jane Hamon has my full respect as a seasoned and trusted prophetess, teacher of the Word and one who is stellar in character. I am fully convinced of the power in the declared word of God and therefore wholeheartedly endorse and recommend *Declarations for Breakthrough*."

Patricia King, author, minister, television host

"Years ago, I learned a great lesson: God's word in my mouth is powerful; to fully activate His word, all I had to do was believe and then speak. In *Declarations for Breakthrough*, Jane Hamon masterfully teaches you how to transform your thinking so that you too can declare breakthroughs for your life, your family, your community and your nation. If you've ever wondered how to achieve the miraculous in your life, get this book, and it will show you how."

Gordon Robertson, president, CBN

"We need and value the Breaker who goes before and breaks open the way! But we need more than that. Too often an individual or a region receives a temporary breakthrough to only end up suffering a terrible setback, resulting in disappointment and a downward spiral. Whew! Anybody have an answer? Jane Hamon gives us some in her new book, *Declarations for Breakthrough*. She gives us the proper reinforcement to create the necessary sustainability! Jane provides us with great structural tools that are needed before and after the change occurs! Thanks, my friend!"

James W. Goll, founder, God Encounters Ministries and
GOLL Ideation LLC; author, communications coach,
recording artist, consultant

"Jane Hamon is one of God's select vessels leading the charge on a timely topic for this season, the power of your decree!

The Lord of the Breakthrough is counseling us, coaching us and instructing us through this book on how to live abundantly in any circumstance. You'll want to read *Declarations for Breakthrough* over and over again. Invest in a few copies, one for you and one for a friend!"

Jennifer Eivaz, co-pastor, Harvest Church, Turlock, California; founder, Harvest Ministries International; author, *Prophetic Secrets* and *Seeing the Supernatural*

"Jane beautifully articulates the power of hearing the voice of God and coming into alignment with His declarations for your life. For anyone wanting a deeper understanding of the power of agreeing with and decreeing God's heart on the earth, this book is for you."

Catherine Mullins, speaker and worship leader

# DECLARATIONS
FOR
# BREAKTHROUGH

# DECLARATIONS
## FOR
# BREAKTHROUGH

### AGREEING WITH THE VOICE OF GOD

# JANE
# HAMON

**Chosen**

a division of Baker Publishing Group
Minneapolis, Minnesota

© 2021 by Jane A. Hamon

Published by Chosen Books
11400 Hampshire Avenue South
Bloomington, Minnesota 55438
www.chosenbooks.com

Chosen Books is a division of
Baker Publishing Group, Grand Rapids, Michigan

Printed in the United States of America

Library of Congress Cataloging-in-Publication Data
Names: Hamon, Jane, author.
Title: Declarations for breakthrough : agreeing with the voice of God / Jane Hamon.
Description: Minneapolis, Minnesota : Chosen Books, a division of Baker Publishing Group, [2021] | Includes bibliographical references.
Identifiers: LCCN 2020044493 | ISBN 9780800761752 (trade paperback) | ISBN 9780800762247 (casebound) | ISBN 9781493429806 (ebook)
Subjects: LCSH: God (Christianity) | Listening—Religious aspects—Christianity. | Prophecies.
Classification: LCC BT103 .H355 2021 | DDC 231.7/45—dc23
LC record available at https://lccn.loc.gov/2020044493

21  22  23  24  25  26  27      7  6  5  4  3  2  1

Dedication
To those who believe our voices can make a difference
as we partner with God to declare His voice
into the earth to bring breakthrough and transformation


In Appreciation
To Tom, my husband of forty years,
for your constant love, support and encouragement
(and for taking me on vacation so I
could get this book written)

# Contents

# Foreword

There is no doubt in my mind that the Body of Christ has entered a new era in God's timetable. I have expected this shift for quite some time, although, like many, I have seen it only "in part." Sometimes we are shown only glimpses of what is coming spiritually; Holy Spirit rarely gives any one person the full picture of where He is taking us. This keeps us seeking His direction, walking by faith. It also reminds us of our need for one another.

Way back in the 1980s I received a prophecy saying that I would be part of "the fresh age of the Melchizedek order." I had no idea at the time what this meant, nor did the person giving me the word! I believe my first thought may have been, *Mel who?* I did, however, study this "king of Salem" and "priest of the Most High God" (Hebrews 7:1) to see if I could glean anything relevant. I learned, among other things, the significance of his being both king and priest, which was rare and very significant. These dual roles, along with other characteristics, made Melchizedek a very important type or picture of Christ, our King and High Priest.

I found this interesting, but still did not know that it fore-shadowed what God would one day elevate His Church into: our kingly and priestly calling.

Kings sit in positions of authority over kingdoms; priests, on the other hand, serve the needs of others. Kings move in authority, releasing it downward from their seat of author-ity; priests offer prayers, petitions, worship and intercession upward on behalf of those they serve. Obviously, Jesus fulfills both of these roles, representing the rule of God to the earth (King) and the needs of humanity to heaven (Priest).

But Christ does not do this alone. Both in the Psalms (110:4) and in the book of Hebrews (5:6, 10; 6:20; 7:1–21), we are told that He would establish a new order or system of priesthood "after the order of Melchizedek." In other words, as both King and Priest, Christ would establish a new order of priests, "a royal priesthood" (1 Peter 2:9). This body of representatives would operate in His dual function of kingly authority and priestly service. Seated spiritually with Him at the right hand of God, they would release commands and declarations on His behalf to the earth; and they would partner with Him in His priestly role of representing the needs of people heavenward.

For generations the Body of Christ has understood our priestly ministry. Prayers, petitions, praise and offerings have ascended to heaven on behalf of ourselves and others. Only recently, however, have we begun to move in our kingly role. This began as a trickle in the '90s as a few believers began making decrees and declarations in their prayers. Suddenly, some Christians were not only talking *to* heaven; they were decreeing *from* heaven! On these shocking occasions, they were not asking for anything; they were binding and loos-ing, commanding doors to open and close, demanding that walls come down and mountains move. A sleeping giant was awakening.

Then, about ten years ago, an understanding began emerging that brought everything into clear focus. Teaching began coming forth regarding the *ekklesia* (the Greek word for "church"). Christians discovered that when Jesus said in Matthew 16:18, "I will build My church [*ekklesia*]," a people the gates of hell could not prevail against, He was referring not to a building, a religious organization, a worship service or even His Bride. He was referring to a legislature, a government body. This was the meaning of the word *ekklesia* in Christ's day.

The game-changer had arrived.

Many in the Body of Christ now realize that we are Christ's governmental arm on the earth. We understand that we have Kingdom authority to speak and command for Him. According to Matthew 16:18–19, we can forbid and allow, bind and loose, command and decree. Christ's arm of government on earth, His *ekklesia*, has been enlightened to our privilege and assignment, and this revelation is resulting in revolutionary change.

As always happens when God restores truth, forerunning voices have been emerging. Apostolic leaders, prophetic leaders and mature teachers are being raised up to instruct the Body of Christ on this all-important subject. One of these voices is that of Jane Hamon. Jane has been a trusted prophetic leader for many years, and it came as no surprise to me that she would give us this sound, seasoned and balanced teaching on the power of declarations. As always with Jane's books, great scholarship mixed with understandability will make it one of the standards on this subject. You will not just read *Declarations for Breakthrough*; you will devour it.

Read it, do it and watch things change!

Dutch Sheets, bestselling author, *Intercessory Prayer* and
many others; founder, *Give Him 15* daily prayer app

# Introduction

"You will also decree a thing, and it will be established for
you; and light will shine on your ways."

Job 22:28 NASB

I love the voice of God. When He speaks, things change. As a
matter of fact, I believe one word from God can change anything and everything. One word from God can change your
family, your health, your finances, your business, your future,
your atmosphere, your community and your nation. When we
agree with the voice of God and verbalize what He is saying,
we are given the power to shift heaven and earth and change
our very circumstances with prophetic declarations. These
authoritative, spiritually empowered decrees have the capacity to bring breakthrough and initiate change.

Psalm 2:7 says, "I will declare the decree." The verb *declare*
means "to make known formally, officially or explicitly."[1] As
a verb, *decree* means "to command, ordain or decide by decree."[2] The noun *decree* used in this verse refers to "a formal
and authoritative order, especially one having the force of law;

[Law:] a judicial decision or order; [Theology:] one of the eternal purposes of God, by which events are foreordained."[3] A *decree* is further defined as "an official statement that something must happen."[4] Daniel 4:17 says, "This decision is by the decree of the watchers." Some matters are decided and determined by speaking powerful declarations, giving voice to decrees that shift heaven and earth.

Decrees have been used for thousands of years by governments as a means to deliver judgments, laws and orders with the expectation that they will be carried out. Esther, Ezra and Daniel are books about decrees being issued that changed the course of history. Such is the governmental Kingdom power God has put into the mouths of His people as we decree what He says!

## "Decree the Abundance of Rain"

My husband, Tom, and I were ministering in Edmonton, Canada, one August during a time when they were experiencing one of the most severe droughts in modern history. They had had a very warm winter and dry spring and had not had rain for months. Because I always check the weather forecasts before arriving in a new city, I knew there were no weather patterns indicating that they could expect any relief. But the first night of our conference, in the middle of my message, I suddenly heard the Lord tell me to decree that the heavens be opened and release the sound of abundance of rain. So I prophesied what I had heard the Lord say, directed the people to shout for joy in response to the word of the Lord, and we pointed our fingers toward the sky while decreeing an abundance of rain.

After agreeing with the voice of God by speaking, decreeing and doing a prophetic act, I shifted back into the message I was giving that night. Fifteen minutes later I noticed that someone came in the back door and whispered to some family members. Those individuals got up and left the service. Soon others came in whispering to their friends and families, and again those individuals got up and left. This was becoming disruptive, so I paused in my ministry and asked what was happening that people were leaving the service.

With big smiles on their faces they began to shout, "It's raining! It's raining!"

We ran quickly to the doors and saw that all those who had left the service were in the parking lot dancing in the rain. Pretty soon, the whole congregation was dancing and declaring, "The drought is over! The drought is over!"

When watching the weather report that night on the local news, we were amused to see that the meteorologists were perplexed, commenting that they had not seen the rain coming. It seemed to come out of nowhere. It rained the whole week we were there.

Several weeks later when we were back home in Florida, the pastor called us. He said, "We are all still rejoicing at how the Lord spoke and decreed an end to our drought. But here is my question. . . . How do you shut it off? It hasn't stopped raining since!"

Clearly God shifted the atmosphere over Edmonton and brought an open heaven through the power of the decree.

## God's Decrees Formed the Universe

In the beginning God formed the worlds through the decrees of His mouth. He said, "Let there be light and there was light." This is the first recorded decree, when God shifted everything by His spoken word. This occurred at a time when the earth was without form and void . . . a wasteland, a desert place filled with chaos, confusion and emptiness. But at the decree from the voice of God, the dark place—filled with misery, death and sorrow—was suddenly transformed into a place of life, with streams of light flowing from our Creator's face, banishing the darkness.

Hebrews 11:3 says, "By faith we understand that the worlds were framed by the word of God, so that the things which are seen were not made of things which are visible." God's words released a creative power that shaped the entire universe. When God speaks, darkness yields to light and death turns to life. His voice is the most powerful force in the universe. It set the sun, the moon and the stars into motion and created the atmosphere over the earth, the water, the sea and dry land. His decrees created plant life, birds, mammals and every living thing that moved on the earth, and it was all very good.

## Jesus Taught the Power of the Decree

When Jesus came to earth, He manifested and demonstrated perfectly all that God had spoken about Himself down through the ages: Jesus, the Word, became flesh. The Greek word for *word* is *logos*.[5] One of the definitions of *logos* is "a decree, mandate or order." Jesus' whole life was a demonstration of God speaking and decreeing His heart and intentions toward mankind.

God told us in the Old Testament that He is the Lord who heals us; Jesus showed us God, the Healer. God told us that He is the God who does wonders; Jesus showed us God, the Miracle Worker. God told us that He is love; Jesus showed us what Love really looks like. It is one thing to hear the voice of the One we love; it is another to see His face. Jesus became the face of the voice of God, so that we can know what it is to experience Him face-to-face.

Throughout His earthly ministry Jesus demonstrated the power of the spoken decree. He told His disciples, "Assuredly, I say to you, if you have faith as a mustard seed, you will *say* to this mountain, 'Move from here to there,' and it will move; and nothing will be impossible for you" (Matthew 17:20, emphasis added).

When He ministered healing and breakthrough to people, He never actually prayed for them "to be healed"; rather, He released declarations of breakthrough, saying things like, "Stretch out your hand; be made whole. . . . Rise, take up your bed and walk." Jesus raised the dead by making decrees: "Lazarus, come forth!" In the situation with Jairus' daughter, He said, "Do not weep. She is not dead; only sleeping. . . . Child, get up." To the dead man at Nain, Jesus decreed, "Young man, I say to you, arise." Matthew 8:16 says that Jesus cast out spirits with a word. To one woman who had suffered from a spirit of infirmity for twelve years He decreed: "Woman, thou art loosed," and she was instantly delivered and healed. When He and His disciples were on a boat and a ferocious storm broke, rather than pray, Jesus made a decree: "Peace, be still!"[6]

## The Early Church—Our Example

Jesus' disciples learned how to use decrees to bring breakthrough to people, setting the example for all believers through the ages. When confronted by the lame man begging for alms at the Beautiful Gate, Peter made a decree that set the man free: "I have no silver or gold, but what I do have I give you. In the name of Jesus Christ of Nazareth, rise up and walk." And the power behind that decree caused that lame man suddenly to jump to his feet, walking and leaping and praising God.[7] These words *rise up* and *walk* are expressed in the imperative mood, not asking permission or making a suggestion, but giving a command.[8]

In Acts 9 we read the story of Dorcas, or Tabitha, a follower of Christ from the city of Lydda, who got very sick and died. Peter came to her and got down on his knees to pray. After praying he turned to her dead body and decreed, "Tabitha, get up." Then she opened her eyes, looked at Peter and sat up.

The apostle Paul also utilized decrees. In Acts 13:11 we read that Paul decreed blindness on Elymas the sorcerer who was hindering the Gospel from going forth. In Acts 14:10 he spoke to a lame man in a loud voice, "Stand up straight on your feet!" And the man leaped up and immediately walked. In Acts 16:18 Paul cast a spirit of divination out of a slave girl who was disrupting the preaching of the Gospel with this decree: "I command you in the name of Jesus Christ to come out of her." And the demon came out that very hour.

Prayer has the power to bring change. James 5:16 tells us that "the heartfelt and persistent prayer of a righteous man (believer) can accomplish much [when put into action and made effective by God—it is dynamic and can have tremendous power]" (AMP). Prayer is actually the foundation for every decree we make, for through a constant flow of communication with the Father, we are able more clearly to hear the words He would have us speak. We pray, connecting to the Father, then we decree, shifting the earth.

We must marry the power of prayer and the authority of the decree. Prayer is our petitions, communication and fellowship with God, while decrees are God's words released through our voices into the earth realm to bring change. These words, which can be Scripture or prophetic words or promises we receive from the Lord, are formed into declarations and spoken out loud. They can be decrees one writes in advance, or spontaneous anointed declarations made in the moment of need.

## The Believer's Decree—Death or Life?

We have seen how God made decrees and formed the worlds out of nothing. We have seen that Jesus made decrees that healed the sick, raised the dead, cast out devils and calmed the storms. We have seen that the first-century disciples also made decrees that brought breakthrough. All of these examples are given in Scripture to show us how to operate in authoritative, governmental decrees in order to break off demonic influence, release supernatural power and extend and expand God's Kingdom rule in the earth.

Job 22:28 begins by saying, "*You* will decree a thing"—not just your pastor, not just a prophet, but *you* shall make decrees that cause things to be established and light to shine on your way. God has put death and life "in the power of the tongue" (Proverbs 18:21). We are, therefore, to "decree a thing." The Hebrew for *thing* (*omer, Strong's* 562) means "the word" or "the promise." What do we decree? We decree what God has spoken.

## The Word of the Lord Brings Life

After a time of ministry in London, England, I arranged to have a free day to take my travel companion around to see some of the sites. At the end of the day, we decided to take in a show at one of London's West End theaters. When the show was over, we all stood to leave, but our path was blocked. People near us were hovering around a man who appeared to be lifeless. The ones tending to him until a medical team could arrive stated that he had no pulse and no breath, and his eyes were fixed and staring. We all assumed he was dead as he was completely unresponsive.

Somehow the crowd parted, and before I even thought about what I was doing I slipped to his side, took his face in my hands, looked straight into his lifeless eyes and said, "Come back now, in Jesus' name."

Nothing seemed to happen, but a woman I assumed was the man's wife began nodding her head and agreeing with my words, speaking in a heavy accent: "Yes, in Jesus' name, in Jesus' name."

So once again I locked my eyes with the man's lifeless eyes and repeated the decree, "Come back now, in Jesus' name." Suddenly, the man blinked, took a deep breath and came back to life! He took my hand and began to shake it and spoke to me emotionally in a language that I did not understand, but I could tell he was thanking me. At that point the authorities in the theater asked everyone please to leave, so I was never able to have a conversation with the man or his wife. But before we left the theater I turned around and saw that she was blowing us kisses, folding her hands together as a sign of prayer and pointing to heaven. She knew that God had just intervened and saved her husband's life.

Today, God is looking for believers who will stay filled with the power of the Holy Spirit so they can boldly declare His life and divine purposes—and change history in a moment. Paul gave us this example when he delivered the slave girl from the demon: He did not stop and pray; he stopped and made a decree. That day in the theater there was no time to pull aside from the chaos and pray to hear God's voice. But because I recognize that the power of the Holy Spirit lives in me, I was able, in an instant, to be used by the Lord to make a declaration that brought breakthrough, even restoring life.

## Decreeing God's Progressive Purposes

Looking once again at the story of Creation, we observe that a series of decrees spoken by the mouth of God formed the worlds. Each word from God built upon the last word from His mouth. On the first day He spoke light into darkness. On the second day He spoke and divided the heavens from the earth. On the third day He spoke and separated the sea from dry land. On and on God spoke, each word building on what He had declared the previous days. In the same way, the word God speaks in one season can form the foundation for what He speaks in subsequent seasons.

Some declarations are given solely for a specific time or event. But sometimes a prophetic declaration inspires people to see the character and nature of God, and the anointing that comes with these declarations can be used at any time. A true prophetic declaration is scripturally based and can, therefore, be drawn upon in subsequent times and seasons.

This book is written to help you understand the power of hearing the voice of the Lord and then to help you write and speak these words as declarations of breakthrough. Each chapter will contain things the Lord has spoken to me and the declarations I have written as a result. I believe these decrees to be founded and grounded in the Word of God and timeless resources to bring breakthrough in your life and circumstances. Open your heart as you read and allow a fresh anointing of the Holy Spirit; open your eyes to see new things; open your ears to hear new things; and open your mind to catapult you into your new season.

--------- YOUR DECLARATION ---------

*I am anointed by the Holy Spirit to release declarations of breakthrough. I have the power to shape my world by the words I speak. I will open my mouth and decree what God says, and things will shift and change for me. I will decree my promises, and they will be established for me, and light will shine on all my ways. I will never stay in darkness, bondage or confusion because my words will break open freedom and revelation. I will always know what God wants me to do and will be empowered to do it because I can hear the voice of God. I have the power of death and life in my tongue; therefore, I will speak life and see breakthrough happen, for me, my family and those I love, even my city and nation. I will make decrees and see God's supernatural power flow from my lips as others are healed, delivered, set free and even raised from the dead. I decree this, in Jesus' name.*

# The Power of Words

"Open your mouth with a mighty decree; I will fulfill it now, you'll see! The words that you speak, so shall it be!"

Psalm 81:10 TPT

Words are powerful. In fact they could be one of the most powerful forces in the universe. In the beginning God spoke and the world and everything in it was formed out of nothing. The invisible became visible because God opened His mouth and spoke. The impossible became possible because God made a decree. God's intentions materialized into reality by the unleashing of His unlimited power through the spoken word. Jesus, who was the very Word made flesh, said, "The words that I speak to you are spirit, and they are life" (John 6:63). His words have the power to bring life to the dead, healing to the sick and freedom to the oppressed. His words have the power to transform the world.

## The Force of God's Voice

Psalm 29:4 tells us, "The voice of the LORD is powerful." The Hebrew word for *powerful* means "force, might, strength, to be firm, full of vigor" (*koakh*, *Strong's* 3581). When God speaks, a powerful force is released that breaks things open and shakes things up. The declarations from God's mouth change everything. When we set our hearts in agreement with what He says, regardless of how impossible it may seem, and speak it out of our own mouths, we become very powerful as well.

Take, for example, a young woman whom my husband, Tom, and I once prophesied to. She had come from a very challenging background and was experiencing a great deal of brokenness in her life. As the Lord spoke to her through us, He addressed things from her past, encouraged her in her present and gave her hope for her future. At no point during the prophecy did God say anything about healing her body; nor did we pray for her healing during our time of ministry. Yet as we prophesied to her, an ear that had been born deaf instantly popped open! Why? Because the voice of the Lord is a force. As God speaks His words to us and through us, unimaginable miracles will result.

Since we are created in God's image, to reflect His nature and operate in His abilities, we possess the same power to create with our words. Our words are a force that has the power to encourage or discourage, to hurt or to heal, to shut down or break open. Proverbs 18:21 in the Passion Translation says, "Your words are so powerful that they will kill or give life," and Proverbs 13:3 says, "Guard your words and you'll guard your life, but if you don't control your tongue, it will ruin everything."

## God's Words in Our Mouths

God once spoke to a young prophet named Jeremiah about the power of the words he would speak.

> Then the LORD put forth His hand and touched my mouth, and the LORD said to me: "Behold, I have put My words in your mouth. See, I have this day set you over the nations and over the kingdoms, to root out and to pull down, to destroy and to throw down, to build and to plant."
>
> Jeremiah 1:9–10

How was Jeremiah going to bring God's government to the earth? How was he anointed to shift nations and kingdoms? By releasing God's words through his mouth that would uproot ungodly structures, systems and spirits and build and plant the new. Jeremiah's words would usher in an entirely different season for the people of God.

Every believer needs to recognize that God longs to put His words in our mouths. God longs to speak clearly to His people so we can in turn say what He is saying. Any time we communicate on earth what God is speaking from heaven, it is prophecy. When we fully embrace the authority He has invested in us through Jesus Christ, we will speak with the weight of the government of the Kingdom of God behind our words, to command and decree a new day and a new way. Our words have power to shift out of an old dysfunctional season into a time of rebuilding, righteousness and renewal. God's words in our mouths are a force that brings healing to the sick, freedom to the oppressed and strength to the weak. The following is a personal story that demonstrates this principle.

## Dabar Shalom

Tom and I have been very blessed with three wonderful children and now seven grandchildren. After the birth of one of our grandchildren, it became apparent he was having challenges. As weeks went by, we noticed he was not progressing the way other children did. He spent most of his waking hours crying as though he was in pain. He cried through the days and the nights, and almost nothing soothed him. He did not make eye contact, roll over or even smile. As the weeks and months went by, doctors began to do tests to determine the underlying issue so we could all know how to help our sweet boy.

When my grandson was five months old, I was on a ministry trip to Trinidad. I was blessed to have an afternoon off from ministry and spent the afternoon in my hotel room praying for God to intervene and bring healing into my grandson's life. I was walking the floor and crying out with all my heart saying, "Lord, please bring healing. Lord, touch his body; touch his life. Whatever is happening with him, I pray You will intervene. Show Your power, Lord. Show Your glory." On and on I prayed in a constant flow of words as my concerns were joined with the power of prayer and intercession in the Holy Spirit.

Suddenly I heard the Lord say, *Shhh! Listen.*

Even though I knew that talking with God should be a two-way street, I was doing all the talking! (Sometimes we need to pray and then listen for God's response.) As I quieted myself, I heard the Lord say this: *Psalm 85:8.* I looked up the verse, which says, "I will hear what God the Lord will speak, for He will speak peace to His people and to His saints." I

28

especially like the wording in the Passion Translation: "Now I'll listen carefully for your voice and wait to hear whatever you say. Let me hear your promise of peace—the message every one of your godly lovers longs to hear."

When God speaks a Scripture to me, I love to dig deep into the meaning of the words. The Hebrew word for *hear* in the line *I will hear what the Lord God will speak* is *shama*, and it means "to hear intelligently often with the implication of attention and obedience, to listen carefully, to listen attentively, to listen intentionally, to discern, to diligently hear, to declare, to proclaim" (*Strong's* 8085). God is challenging us to listen intentionally and to hear intelligently in order to receive His strategies for victory. Breakthrough has its beginning and ending in hearing the voice of the Lord.

The Scripture goes on to say, "He will speak peace to His people." The phrase *speak peace* in Hebrew is *dabar shalom*. *Dabar* means "to speak, to declare, to proclaim, to issue a command, to promise" (*Strong's* 1696). Within this word is the concept of God releasing a declaration or command that changes things. What is God declaring? Peace. Most believers have heard the word *shalom* and know it to be a Jewish greeting or blessing bestowed on someone. The word *shalom*, however, has a much deeper meaning. It does mean peace, but it also means "tranquility, wholeness, completeness, health, wealth, prosperity, favor, the ability to finish, to be safe" (*Strong's* 7965). Someone once said it carries the connotation of nothing missing, nothing broken, nothing damaged. What a promise! What a decree!

I flew home the next day, and on the following Sunday we decided to declare *dabar shalom* over our grandson during the service. After the time of worship, we brought him to the front and explained to our congregation that he was seemingly delayed in his development. I then explained that the Lord had given me the verse about *dabar shalom*. So we held him up to the Lord and decreed peace, wholeness, completeness, health and blessing. Do you know our grandson had the nerve to scream and cry all the way through our anointed decrees for peace? After the prayer his parents took him quickly back to the nursery, and he continued to cry the whole way.

That day after church the family all came to our house for lunch. At one point my grandson's mommy put him down on a blanket to change his clothes, and guess what? He did not cry. This was the first time any of us could remember that he was put down without crying, so we were all looking at him and celebrating.

Then as we all watched, he suddenly rolled over. He had never rolled over before, yet just a couple hours after the declaration of *shalom* he was rolling over. His mom picked him up, and he made eye contact and gave her a big smile. More firsts! Within a short period of time of declaring the *shalom* of God over him—wholeness, completeness, health and peace—our grandson made huge advancements in his development, which continues to be evidenced year by year as he grows.

## The Power of the Mouth

Throughout Scripture we are taught that when God speaks, things happen. Isaiah 30:31, for instance, says that the voice of the Lord shatters the Assyrians (the enemy). Many believers fail to understand, however, that when God speaks on earth He often chooses to do it through human mouths. In the Old Testament God spoke through the mouths of the prophets: Moses, David, Elijah and Elisha, Isaiah and Jeremiah, to name just a few. Kingdoms rose and fell by the power of the words of the prophets, the mouths of His anointed ones.

Here are just a few familiar Old Testament examples that show how God used the power of the spoken word to shift heaven and earth.

### 1. Creation

Genesis 1 records the first declarations from God's mouth, which resulted in the six days of creation of the earth, the heavens and everything in them. After the creation of man, God gave Adam his first assignment, which involved using his mouth to name all the animals. Every one of us is created in God's image and after His likeness; therefore, we have the same creative, declarative power in the words we speak.

### 2. The Tower of Babel

Genesis 11 relates the story of corporate rebellion against God. The earth had only one language at the time, which resulted in an unprecedented unity, although it was unity in rebellion. Genesis 11:6 says this: "And the Lord said, 'Indeed the people are one and they all have one language, and this is what they begin to do; now nothing that they propose to do will be withheld from them.'" So God scattered the people by confusing their language and breaking their dangerous unity. Today, God has given a common language back to His Church, the language of the Holy Spirit, which will result in even greater power and unity for the building of the Kingdom of God in the earth.

### 3. The Burning Bush

Moses was chosen by God to deliver Israel out of Egyptian bondage. In Exodus 3–4, we read that God addressed Moses through a burning bush. Moses at this point was living on the back side of the desert, full of shame from killing an Egyptian soldier in a futile, fleshly attempt to free God's people by his own strength. God spoke to Moses and called him back to the frontline of service—to go before Pharaoh and say on God's behalf, "Let My people go." Moses, who by his own admission was slow of speech, argued with God that perhaps he was not the best choice. God responded by saying, "Who has made man's mouth? . . . Have not I the LORD? Now therefore, go, and I will be with your mouth and teach you what you shall say" (Exodus 4:11–12). This promise is for each of us today as we endeavor to speak and decree God's purposes into the earth. He will be with our mouths and teach us what we are to say.

### 4. The Plagues in Egypt

In Exodus 7–11 we have the biblical account of the ten plagues in Egypt. God spoke to Moses and instructed him to declare each plague to Pharaoh before it occurred. Notice, it was not until Moses spoke that the plagues were released. Moses' declarations turned water to blood, released pestilence and hail, and even foretold the deaths of the firstborn. God directed Moses to decree these drastic measures in order to see Israel set free. As New Testament believers, our first calling is to speak life and release blessings; however, there may be times when a prophetic word is spoken to indicate God's judgment, particularly over a city or nation (for the purpose of bringing a future opportunity for freedom).

### 5. Balaam's Donkey

Balaam was a self-willed prophet who was asked by the messengers of an enemy king to come use his powers to curse Israel (see Numbers 22). Tempted by the king's offer, Balaam set out, but along the way the Angel of the Lord stood in his path with a drawn sword to prevent him from going further.

Balaam's donkey, who apparently had more discernment than Balaam, saw the angel and refused to move forward. As Balaam beat the donkey repeatedly, God opened her mouth and she spoke to Balaam, making an appeal to him regarding the abuse. This supernatural event did not faze Balaam. He was repentant only after the Lord opened his eyes and said that if it had not been for the donkey he would be dead. Sometimes God may speak through the most unexpected person or circumstance to try to turn us from our own self-willed paths and get us back on track with God.

### 6. The Walls of Jericho

In Joshua 6 we read the story of the siege of Jericho. The Lord gave Joshua a strategy to take the city—which sounds to the natural mind fairly ridiculous. He was to have his army march around Jericho one time every day for six days. Only the sound of seven priests blasting seven trumpets of rams' horns was to be heard. On the seventh day they were to march around the city seven times with the seven trumpets of rams' horns sounding. On the final trip around, the priests were to make long blasts with a ram's horn, and at that signal, all the people were to give a great shout. When they shouted, the Lord's promise was that the walls would fall down flat.

It sounded impossible, but Israel followed the command. They were probably asked to remain silent until the final day because of their tendency to murmur and complain; the power of those words would have cost them their victory. (How often do we talk ourselves out of the victory God has promised by our own words of doubt and unbelief?) Instead of talking they were to listen to the sound of the trumpets, which represented the voice of the Lord. When we allow the voice of the Lord to fill our heart and minds, faith will arise. When the people finally released the shout of victory from their mouths, the mighty walls of Jericho crumbled and fell. Their mouths released their breakthrough. Breakthrough has a sound, and it comes from the mouths of those who have heard the voice of the Lord.

### 7. The Sun Standing Still

In Joshua 10 we find that Joshua spoke to the Lord, then spoke to the sun and moon and commanded them to stay still so he could complete the battle.

> Then Joshua spoke to the LORD in the day when the LORD delivered up the Amorites before the children of Israel, and he said in the sight of Israel: "Sun, stand still over Gibeon; and Moon, in the Valley of Aijalon." So the sun stood still, and the moon stopped, till the people had revenge upon their enemies. Is this not written in the Book of Jasher? So the sun stood still in the midst of heaven, and did not hasten to go down for about a whole day. And there has been no day like that, before it or after it, that the LORD heeded the voice of a man; for the LORD fought for Israel.
>
> Joshua 10:12–14

God heeded the voice of a man and then fought for his nation. Wow! Just think about the power and authority given to believers when we align with heaven and speak His purposes into the earth.

This is by no means an exhaustive list but is shared to remind us that God has used the mouths of His people from the beginning of time to effect change and bring victory. God needs our mouths to preach the Gospel as well as to release His supernatural power throughout the earth.

## New Testament Power

In the New Testament we see that God's plan was to release even greater authority through the mouths of His people. He now desires to speak not only through prophets or other ministers but also through the mouths of an entire prophetic generation of people who are filled with His Holy Spirit.

Acts 2 tells us that on the Day of Pentecost believers were gathered in one accord in an upper room when suddenly the room was filled with the sound of a rushing mighty wind. Flames of fire were seen on the heads of the disciples, and they were all filled with the Holy Spirit. The initial evidence of this infilling was that each disciple opened his or her mouth, and a language of the Spirit began to pour forth. This was the pure utterance of the Holy Spirit, God Himself, speaking out of the mouths of believers, manifesting His presence and power.

After they spilled out of the room where they had been waiting, the crowds of foreigners gathering for the Feast of Pentecost in the streets of Jerusalem heard the Gospel preached in their own native tongues. Peter stood up and explained that this experience had been foretold by the prophet Joel.

"But this is what was spoken by the prophet Joel: 'And it shall come to pass in the last days, says God, that I will pour out of My Spirit on all flesh; your sons and your daughters shall prophesy, your young men shall see visions, your old men shall dream dreams. And on My menservants and on My maidservants I will pour out My Spirit in those days; and they shall prophesy.'"

Acts 2:16–18

Once the outpouring of the Holy Spirit came, not only would people experience revelation through dreams and visions, but God would put His words in their mouths and they would prophesy. God's intentions were that His people would release declarations empowered by revelation that would bring Kingdom breakthrough into the earth.

## The Heart/Mouth Connection

Have you ever heard something come out of your mouth that shocked you? In an effort to explain the statement away, you might say, "I don't know why I said that." When Jesus was talking to His disciples about producing good "fruit" in their lives, He said, "Out of the abundance of the heart [the] mouth speaks" (Luke 6:45). He was saying that one can measure what is in one's heart based on the words spoken. So if you hear some random statement come out of your mouth that seems to come from nowhere, it is actually coming from somewhere—hidden somewhere in your heart. The heart informs what the mouth speaks.

In the spirit realm there is a powerful connection between what the heart believes and what the mouth speaks. As a matter of fact, in order to attain salvation it is not enough to believe in our hearts that Jesus is the Son of God; we must also open our mouths and actually speak forth that truth. Paul outlined this clearly.

> But what does it say? "The word is near you, in your mouth and in your heart" (that is, the word of faith which we preach): that if you confess with your mouth the Lord Jesus and believe in your heart that God has raised Him from the dead, you will be saved. For with the heart one believes unto righteousness, and with the mouth confession is made unto salvation.
>
> Romans 10:8–10

This is a principle that can be applied to anything we desire from the Lord, or to anything God would have us release into the earth. The mouth activates what the heart believes. If we truly believe that God is a healer, then we must open our mouths and declare it. Our words can activate healing in our own lives or in others'. If we truly believe God wants to bless us and provide for us, it is not sufficient merely to meditate on those thoughts; rather, we must confess what we believe out loud by declaring His Word and His promises.

Neither is it sufficient to speak words without faith in our hearts. Empty words, even if chanted repeatedly, have no power to bring change. We can say the right words, sing the right songs, talk the right talk, but if our hearts are not actively engaging our faith, it will not produce the fruit we desire. Quoting Isaiah, Jesus said this of the Jewish leaders of His day: "These people draw near to Me with their mouth, and honor Me with their lips, but their heart is far from Me" (Matthew 15:8).

Rather we should be like David, who was a lover of God in his heart but also expressed that love through extravagant words, such as when he said, "Let the words of my mouth and the meditation of my heart be acceptable in Your sight, O LORD, my strength and my Redeemer" (Psalm 19:14).

Second Corinthians 4:13 affirms this as well: "First I believed, then I spoke in faith" (TPT).

The beauty of the heart/mouth connection is that one can strengthen the other. Romans 10:17 says that "faith comes by hearing, and hearing by the word of God." As we open our mouths and declare the word of God audibly (both Scripture as well as words of revelation that agree with those words), our ability to believe what we say through faith begins to grow.

As we read Scripture and pray out loud (not just silently), the voice of God is released into the atmosphere surrounding our lives and circumstances. Things begin to change every bit as much as when God initially spoke and said, "Let there be light!" As we sing worship songs that are scripturally based and join our faith to what we are singing, our songs become decrees that have the power for breakthrough. Psalm 149:6–9 speaks of the power of our praise when it declares:

> Let the high praises of God be in their mouth, and a two-edged sword in their hand, to execute vengeance on the nations, and punishments on the peoples; to bind their kings with chains, and their nobles with fetters of iron; to execute on them the written judgment— this honor have all His saints. Praise the LORD!

Our high praise has governmental power when we open our mouths and declare His divine purposes through song.

Moses, when addressing the Israelites, emphasized this principle:

> "The word is very near you, in your mouth and in your heart, that you may do it. See, I have set before you today life and good, death and evil, in that I command you today to love the LORD your God, to walk in His ways, and to keep His commandments, His statutes, and His judgments, that you may live and multiply; and the LORD your God will bless you in the land which you go to possess. . . . I call heaven and earth as witnesses today against you, that I have set before you life and death, blessing and cursing; therefore choose life, that both you and your descendants may live; that you may love the LORD your God, that you may obey His voice, and that you may cling to Him, for He is your life and the length of your days; and that you may dwell in the land which the LORD swore to your fathers, to Abraham, Isaac, and Jacob, to give them."
>
> Deuteronomy 30:14–16, 19–20

These blessings all begin by allowing God's word to be both in our hearts and in our mouths.

## The Science Behind Self-Talk

Do you ever talk to yourself? Out loud? Have you ever been told that people who talk to themselves are a bit crazy? Science is beginning to find just the opposite in new studies on the subject of self-talk. Self-talk is how one talks about oneself both internally as well as out loud, and it has the power to shape one's life. It comes out of internal dialogue, which is largely influenced by thoughts, perspectives, experiences, faith and belief systems.

Studies have proven the value of positive self-talk on the performance of students, athletes, salespeople and even children. People who have a positive internal self-talk, which is then verbalized, experience greater strength, enjoyment and long-term success. Some studies suggest that positive self-talk can result in a vast array of physical and mental health benefits including "increased vitality, improved immune function, reduced pain, better cardiovascular health, reduced risk for death and less stress and distress."[1] On the other hand, those with negative or critical self-talk tend to experience greater anxiety, fear, shame, physical and mental health issues and limitations.[2]

Dr. Caroline Leaf, author of the bestselling *Switch On Your Brain* and other books, writes:

Breakthrough neuroscientific research is confirming daily what we instinctively knew all along: what you are thinking every moment of every day becomes a physical reality in your brain and body, which affects your optimal mental and physical health. These thoughts collectively form your attitude, which is your state of mind, and it's your attitude and not your DNA that determines much of the quality of your life.[3]

In other words, we can control our lives by controlling how we think!

In 1 Samuel 30 we observe this concept in the life of David, who was anointed but not yet crowned to be king of Israel. At one point, as he and his men were away from their camp and preparing to enter into battle, the Amalekites swept into the camp and took the wives, children and belongings of David and all his men.

When they discovered this, a cry of grief went up from among his soldiers, and there was angry talk of stoning him. David was greatly distressed. But at that moment David did two things: He engaged in positive self-talk by encouraging himself in the Lord, and then he enquired of the Lord (see 1 Samuel 30:6–8). David understood that as he encouraged himself by causing his soul to bless the Lord, he was bringing his thoughts into alignment with how God thinks. God then gave him a strategy to pursue, overtake and recover all. The Israelites not only overtook their enemy and received back everything that had been stolen, but they also acquired a great deal of spoil. Had David not encouraged himself in the Lord first, he might not have had the faith to act on the word of the Lord when it came. There is a clear connection between David stewarding his thought life and bringing victory to the entire camp.

## Renewing Our Minds

Proverbs 23:7 tells us that "as [someone] thinks in his heart, so is he." The connection between how we think and what we speak affects our experiences in life. The book of Proverbs is rich in wisdom concerning this connection and how it affects body, soul and spirit: "Anxiety weighs down the heart of a man, but a good word cheers it up" (Proverbs 12:25 BSB); "Pleasant words are a honeycomb, sweet to the soul and healing to the bones" (Proverbs 16:24 NASB). The right words can bring healing to both soul and body.

If the words we speak are influenced by what we think, we must renew our minds continually in order to think the way God thinks. Paul encourages us to "be transformed by the renewing" of our minds (Romans 12:2). The Passion Translation says it this way:

> Stop imitating the ideals and opinions of the culture around you, but be inwardly transformed by the Holy Spirit through a total reformation of how you think. This will empower you to discern God's will as you live a beautiful life, satisfying and perfect in his eyes.

We renew our minds by thinking about the right things, guarding what our eyes and ears take in, taking captive vain imaginations and rejecting negativity. Our minds are transformed when we allow God's Word to wash over us on a regular basis—allowing us to detoxify from the influence of the world around us. When we begin to think as God thinks, we will begin to say what God says.

This transformation has the power to change not only our lives but also the lives of those around us. A guarded thought life will result in a fountain of vitality and beauty flowing from our lips. Ephesians 4:29 encourages us with these words: "Never let ugly or hateful words come from your mouth, but instead let your words become beautiful gifts that encourage others; do this by speaking words of grace to help them" (TPT). Our words have power to transform lives.

All of this is vital for understanding the power of declarations. The words we speak are powerful and have the capacity to shape our world. For this reason, the more Christlike our thought processes are, the more apt we are to speak words that shift death into life. We are God's ambassadors in this world, and what we speak and declare causes His Kingdom to come and His will to be done, on earth as it is in heaven.

## YOUR DECLARATION

*I declare that God has put His words into my mouth. Because Christ is in me, my words are also spirit and life. When I speak, I can change my world. My words are powerful and Spirit-filled. When I speak, miracles happen. My thoughts are focused on what is pure, lovely, just and virtuous. I will speak that which is life-giving and not death-dealing. I will encourage myself in the Lord and accomplish His will for my life. I am strong. I am able. I am more than a conqueror because He loves me. I dabar shalom, decreeing the peace of God over my life: nothing missing, nothing broken, nothing damaged. I will pursue, overtake and recover all that the enemy has robbed from me. I hear God speaking to me in this verse: "Open your mouth with a mighty decree; I will fulfill it now, you'll see! The words that you speak, so shall it be! (Psalm 81:10 TPT).*

## YOUR ACTIVATION

1. Can you identify any pessimistic thought pattern or self-talk that is causing negative words to come from your mouth? Examples are: *I am not good-looking enough. I am not smart enough. I am not brave*

*enough. I can't hear God's voice. I will never be good enough.* Find several Scriptures to meditate on to help change this pattern.

2. Is there an area of your life that you are limiting by negative self-talk? Examples are: *I will never succeed. I am always broke. I am a failure. I could never do that.* Take some time to listen to the Lord and write what you hear Him say about that area of your life. I believe you will discover that God's voice sounds just the opposite of those statements. Now determine to say what God says about you and replace the limiting statements with new, positive ones.

3. Can you identify any area of your life in which you are not experiencing the fullness of what you know God has for you? Perhaps it is your family/marriage relationship, finances, health, business or ministry calling. Shape your world by your words through writing and speaking a decree. Using the Scriptures you meditated on in #1 above and the statements you wrote for #2, write a decree.

# The Power of Decrees

My wonderful God, you are to be praised above all; teach me the power of your decrees!

Psalm 119:12 TPT

Tom and I are blessed to have lived in the beautiful panhandle of Florida for several decades. We came here before many of the resorts, restaurants and shopping centers were built. In fact, when we first arrived it was a forty-minute drive to the nearest gas station and grocery store. Even though we lived about three miles from some of the most beautiful beaches in the world, it seemed as though our area was trapped in a perpetual cycle of poverty. As pastors who were also inter-cessors for our area, Tom and I noticed new businesses open only to close a short time later. Development projects were begun and then abandoned. We even knew people who built homes, only to lose them in foreclosure within a few years. It seemed as if we were fighting an unseen force that had our area locked up in poverty, and we were determined to work with the Lord to see things change.

We organized teams that walked each street and neighborhood of our area, praying, decreeing blessings and breakthrough over every home and business. We also had research teams look into the history of our land for any insight into how we needed to pray to see it unlocked.

These researchers discovered several things for us to pray about that could have contributed spiritually to the entrenched poverty. They uncovered curses recorded by the indigenous people who were driven off the land hundreds of years before; piracy activity along our beaches; organized crime connections in the earliest businesses in the area; and active occult and witchcraft groups. But they also discovered an obscure reference in our county record books that named South Walton County "Poor Man's Island." We realized that the enemy had released a decree over our territory that was acting as a spiritual force holding curses in place and prosperity captive.

So we wrote a different decree. We named our area the "Land of Blessing and Favor" and declared it when we walked and prayed through the neighborhoods. Just as Jeremiah's calling was to uproot and pull down so that Israel could build and plant (see Jeremiah 1:10), we realized that our job was to uproot the old decree of the enemy and instead plant God's decree for our land.

Now, after decades of praying and decreeing over our land, we are one of the most prosperous counties in Florida. We watched as the area went from struggling to surviving to thriving.

It is important to understand the process of a divine decree in order to embrace fully the authority God has entrusted to us. Ancient kings, who spoke with power, issued decrees in order to enact laws and policies. When a king made a decree, everyone within his jurisdiction had to submit or face the consequences. The release of a decree set a whole governmental process into motion. The Bible has numerous examples of kings making decrees: We see examples in the books of Ezra and Nehemiah, which describe the rebuilding of the Temple and the city of Jerusalem. Esther, Daniel and Jonah all acknowledged the power of a king's decree.

## 1. God Decrees His Intentions

When God creates a land or a people, He has a specific purpose and plan in mind. Certain inherent qualities of His goodness and grace are instilled into every culture. Psalm 119:91 says, "By your decree everything stands at attention, for all that you have made serves you" (TPT). God did not decree our area to be "Poor Man's Island" but rather a land of blessing. Our prayers broke the alignment in the spirit to the false decree and established God's original decree for the land, releasing it to prosper as intended.

So it is with releasing the voice of the Lord through prophecy. God loves to speak to people about His original intent and plan. He wants to see His decree over a person's life come to fruition, regardless of what that person has experienced.

I once prophesied over a young woman that God had created her to be a voice for justice and to bring His principles into the earth through an anointing for government. Sadly, because she had experienced a great deal of abuse and injustice in her life, she had never believed that she could be a voice for change. She had never seen any way that her life would possibly make a difference. But as the prophetic word went over her, God's original decree began to resonate within her. She wanted to make a difference. She wanted to be a change-maker.

She aligned with God's decree, sought healing for her hurts, re-engaged with the education process and later got involved in government, first on the local level and then on the national level. God's prophetic decree awakened her to her destiny.

## 2. Decrees Set Progress in Motion

When God gives a decree, everything shifts to accommodate His will. When Jesus declared "Peace, be still!" to the storm, all heaven shifted causing a corresponding shift in the earth realm. How does God decree things in the earth today? Through the mouths of His people who discern His will and intentions and speak them forth, bringing breakthrough.

On one occasion I was ministering in Guatemala. On the first night God impressed me to prophesy and decree that He was bringing exposure to a child sex-trafficking ring. The prophecy included these words: "Even now I am putting things in place to bring exposure and justice in this land." Several days later, headlines revealed that the U.S. government had issued many arrests and freed hundreds of children who were caught in an organized trafficking ring. The voice of the Lord foretells what is to come, and as the declarations are released the words set things into motion in the realm of the spirit.

Scripture declares that "surely the Lord GOD does nothing, unless He reveals His secret to His servants the prophets" (Amos 3:7). God loves to reveal His plans to us—desiring that we speak them out and, by doing so, pull His intentions out of the spirit realm and manifest breakthrough in the natural realm. When we decree God's plan by speaking it out of our mouths, it sets His plans in motion.

Some years ago the Lord spoke to me that we have entered a "Cyrus season" of breakthrough. I wrote a book exploring how God used that Persian king to release a decree that fulfilled ancient prophecy for the Jews and changed the course of history.[1] The Cyrus decree brought not only freedom from bondage but also the necessary resources, weaponry and authority to accomplish the restoration of the Temple and the rebuilding of Jerusalem. His decree opened the heavens and opened the earth. I believe we are living in a similar time in which God is fulfilling long-standing prophecies and bringing breakthrough.

To understand this more fully we must remember Jewish history. Because of a pattern of disobedience toward God, Judah was taken away into Babylonian captivity. God had spoken to them through the prophet Isaiah about a man who would be raised up and deliver them from their bondage, even identifying him by name: Cyrus. One of the most incredible things about this prophecy is that Isaiah spoke it some two hundred years before God used Cyrus to liberate the Jews. Here is Isaiah's declaration about Cyrus:

> "Thus says the LORD to His anointed, to Cyrus, whose right hand I have held—to subdue nations before him and loose the armor of kings, to open before him the double doors, so that the gates will not be shut: 'I will go before you and make the crooked places straight; I will break in pieces the gates of bronze and cut the bars of iron. I will give you the treasures of darkness and hidden riches of secret places, that you may know that I, the LORD, who call you by your name, am the God of Israel. For Jacob My servant's sake, and Israel My elect, I have even called you by your name; I have named you, though you have not known Me.'"
>
> Isaiah 45:1–4

The prophecy goes on to describe a ruler who will rebuild God's city and set the captives free.

Daniel was a leader of God's people during the Babylonian captivity and pored over the Scriptures in order to pray God's prophesied purposes forth. He knew that the prophecy of Isaiah identified the deliverer by name, so when Babylon was conquered by Cyrus the Great, Daniel likely read the prophecy to the new ruler describing what the God of heaven had created him to accomplish.

Cyrus would have discovered his personal destiny in the prophecy of Isaiah. God had broken the way open for him to overthrow Babylon and called him by his name, even though Cyrus did not know Him. As a result he obeyed the word of the Lord and released the Jewish captives, put weapons and wealth in their hands and authorized them by decree to go back and build God's house in Jerusalem.

The book of Ezra records this decree, which was a legislative order to set new policies and procedures in motion.

> Now in the first year of Cyrus king of Persia, that the word of the Lord by the mouth of Jeremiah might be fulfilled, the Lord stirred up the spirit of Cyrus king of Persia, so that he made a proclamation throughout all his kingdom, and also put it in writing, saying, Thus says Cyrus king of Persia: All the kingdoms of the earth the Lord God of heaven has given me. And He has commanded me to build Him a house at Jerusalem which is in Judah. Who is among you of all His people? May his God be with him, and let him go up to Jerusalem which is in Judah, and build the house of the Lord God of Israel (He is God), which is in Jerusalem.
>
> Ezra 1:1–3

For more than seventy years the Jewish people had been in slavery in Babylon (see Jeremiah 25:12). When Cyrus released this decree, this proclamation of freedom, they were instantly set free. The decree changed everything! A whole new chapter in history was begun. Many of the Jews packed up their belongings and returned to Jerusalem immediately and embarked on the mission to build God's house. They quickly laid the foundation of the Temple and had an incredible time of worship, celebrating that God's restoration process had begun.

### 3. The Enemy Issues Counter Decrees

When God issues a decree setting His divine purposes in motion, we need to be aware that the enemy usually issues a decree to stop the progress. God is the originator, initiator and creator; the enemy is only an imitator and counterfeiter. The enemy's decrees, therefore, will sound like the opposite of God's decrees. The enemy loves to hijack God's purposes, those that are fair and just, and declare the opposite. Isaiah spoke a word about those who defy God's laws: "Woe to those who decree unrighteous decrees, who write misfortune, which they have prescribed" (Isaiah 10:1). The devil's plan is to keep a population oppressed and operating under decrees of death rather than fulfilling God's intention for life and freedom.

As the Jews continued to build the Temple under the authority of Cyrus' decree, they faced a spirit of resistance in counter decrees. Ezra records this: "Then the people of the land tried to discourage the people of Judah. They troubled them in building, and hired counselors against them to frustrate their purpose all the days of Cyrus king of Persia, even until the reign of Darius king of Persia" (Ezra 4:4–5).

The forces of darkness love to stir up trouble and frustrate—"shatter, divide or break apart" (*parar, Strong's* 6565)— the purposes of God and His people. When that happens, we can lose sight of God's original decree. Sometimes it is easiest to identify it again by looking at the enemy's decree given in response to it: The enemy's decree is always the opposite of God's original decree. If, for instance, a territory—or even a person's life—is overtaken by poverty, injustice and destruction, you can be sure that God's intention is for prosperity, justice and life.

In this case, Ezra 4:21 tells us that a decree was made to cause all forward progress of rebuilding in the city to stop, and this included the rebuilding of the Temple (see verse 24). God's decree was "build"; the enemy's decree was "stop."

When Tom and I first moved here, we found the surrounding area not only bound by poverty from the decree of "Poor Man's Island" but also inundated with every form of witchcraft, occultism and paganism. You see, God had decreed that this land would be a place where the modern-day prophetic movement would be birthed and established, so the enemy released his own claim. In order for us to see the destiny of our land released, we had to reclaim our territory for God's Kingdom purposes and also break the hold of the false claims, for they empowered demonic structures.

When you observe that the enemy has released decrees over a person or family, such as abuse, injustice, addiction, dysfunction, poverty, lack, religion, unbelief, pride, shame, premature death, covenant breaking leading to divorce, etc., then you must break any agreement with these decrees and instead listen to and proclaim what God has decreed—just as Zerubbabel and his builders continued to press through the opposition.

### 4. Prophetic Voices Reactivate God's Decrees

Though Cyrus had decreed building the Temple, the subsequent decrees to stop made by Israel's enemies—those discouraging, frustrating words—also held authority, and the work ceased. This gives us an important example when it comes to reactivating a decree that has been lying dormant. Sometimes the circumstances of life press in on us and cause us to lose sight of what God has spoken. In times like these we must listen for the prophetic voice of God to bring us back into alignment with His will and plan.

In Ezra 5, which addresses the effort to build under Darius, we see that the voice of the Lord caused the people to reengage with God's plan. After a pause in building, the prophets began to speak and reactivate the original decree.

> When the prophets, Haggai the prophet and Zechariah the son of Iddo, prophesied to the Jews who were in Judah and Jerusalem in the name of the God of Israel, who was over them, then Zerubbabel the son of Shealtiel and Jeshua the son of Jozadak arose and began to rebuild the house of God which is in Jerusalem; and the prophets of God were with them supporting them.
>
> Ezra 5:1–2 NASB

As they began to build again, the same spirit of resistance arose from political leaders, who sent a letter to King Darius, questioning whether or not a decree was ever given to rebuild the Temple (see Ezra 5:17). When challenged about this, Zerubbabel had explained to these leaders that the original decree was indeed true.

Darius decreed that such a search be conducted, and Cyrus' decree was found. The king's response to those resisting the building of the Temple was this: "Let the work of this house of God alone; let the governor of the Jews and the elders of the Jews build this house of God on its site" (Ezra 6:7).

The reactivation of the original decree came because the prophets prophesied. The voice of the Lord, whether through a prophet, or through the Holy Spirit speaking personally to us, will often challenge us to remember what God said in a previous season. We have a saying around our church, "Never doubt in the dark what you heard in the light." In other words, when we face trials or difficulties we need to remember what God spoke before the trouble started. When we are faced with a negative report that wants to stop our progress, we must go back to God's word and previous prophecies and search it out, like searching the royal treasuries, to find the previous, original decree.

If you receive a report of sickness, search the royal treasuries of God's Word to find the original decree: "By His stripes I am healed" (see Isaiah 53:5). If you face a time of financial difficulty, search the royal treasuries of God's Word to find what God first said: "God has given me the power to get wealth" (see Deuteronomy 8:18). If you face a time of confusion or mental duress, search the royal treasuries of God's Word and find the original decree: "Now may the Lord of peace Himself give me peace always in every way" (see 2 Thessalonians 3:16).

As we interceded over our land to break poverty we discovered the enemy's decree. So we began diligently to declare the opposite, and we have seen prosperity manifest.

This is why, whenever I travel, I find it valuable to listen in the Spirit to hear what God has declared over a region. Then I can work with the leaders and people of that region to deactivate the decree of hell and reactivate God's decree. Sometimes I hear God's decree by the Spirit, and sometimes I am instructed to research a particular part of history of the land. At times I hear the Lord's decree in the national or state motto or in a phrase used by the people who live there.

I was ministering in Glasgow, Scotland, when I heard the Lord say that the land was "a healing well" and that God was breaking that well open once again. I asked David and Emma

Stark, strong prophetic leaders in Scotland, about the history of Glasgow and learned that a man known as Saint Mungo had a well recognized for its healing water. It was one of the last places on earth that miracles and healings occurred in the Church prior to the Dark Ages. God was opening up the well of healing and causing the area to be known again as a place of miracles.

But the Starks also told me that the nickname of Glasgow is the "Sick Man of Europe" due to high mortality rates as well as suicides. God's decree was miracles; the enemy's counter decree was sickness and death.[2]

While traveling near Buffalo, New York, I heard God decree that that area was created to be a spiritual womb, birthing awakening and revival for the United States. As I began to research how this might have manifested in the natural, I read that Upstate New York was instrumental in the Second Great Awakening, seeing entire cities turn to Christ. This awakening also inspired the Fulton Street (New York City) Prayer Revival, which reached around the globe. This region was created to facilitate worldwide revival!

But I also learned that the enemy had hijacked the decree of being a spiritual womb: In 1848 the Fox sisters of Hydesville, in Western New York State, introduced the occult practice of spiritualism, or communication with the dead. This practice spread around the world from the Buffalo area in a short period of time.[3] In addition, Joseph Smith, founder of Mormonism, claimed to have encountered the angel Moroni in 1823 at his home in Palmyra, also in Western New York State, giving rise to the Church of Jesus Christ of Latter-day Saints.

God's decree was for this region to be a place of revival and awakening, not of birthing organizations with false doctrine and occult practices. In both this instance and the guidance we were given in Scotland, I believe that God was issuing a challenge for the people of those regions to align with His original decree and see His plan reactivated in the land.

## 5. God's Reactivated Decree Gains in Power

The book of Ezra opens with Cyrus issuing a decree of freedom and restoration for the people of God. They began strong, excited about the new season God was bringing them into. But then they hit troubled times when the enemy issued counter decrees to stop their advancement. After a period of time the prophets began to speak, awakening the authority to align with the original decree. Then the most amazing thing happened: The decree gained in power.

Once Darius reinstated the legal decree of Cyrus, all the previous conditions came back into play; however, now he issued an additional decree, increasing the scope and magnitude of the original. Darius stated:

> Moreover I issue a decree as to what you shall do for the elders of these Jews, for the building of this house of God: Let the cost be paid at the king's expense from taxes on the region beyond the River; this is to be given immediately to these men, so that they are not hindered.
>
> Ezra 6:8

Cyrus' decree gave them authority to be set free from slavery, to rebuild the Temple, and to take a free will offering with them as they returned home. Now Darius said to take the taxes from that region and use the money to build without hindrance. He added that anyone who interfered with this mission would be killed. Wow! That is authority!

In Ezra 7 we find that, in time, a new king by the name of Artaxerxes came to power. The king learned of the rebuilding the Jews were accomplishing, including with the Temple. But Ezra was serving in the king's court, and Scripture says that "the good hand of his God" was upon Ezra. He—and the plight of the Jews—found favor with the king (Ezra 7:9).

Now, not to be outdone by his predecessors, Artaxerxes gave an even greater release of power, authority and wealth through his decree to continue building the city and complete any work on the Temple. He authorized Ezra to go help the Israelites, and to take with him all the gold and silver the king and his advisors were sending with him, all the gold and silver from free will offerings of the people, and finally all the gold and silver he could obtain from all the providence of Babylon. Not only did this decree authorize a huge wealth transfer, but it also authorized Ezra to appoint magistrates, judges and teachers who knew the law of God. The decree released wealth, governmental power to legislate and authority to preach the word—and it caused the work of restoration to be complete.

### 6. A Decree Is an Invisible Force

Here is another important thing to realize about the process of the decree: When a decree is made, there is a shift in the spiritual realm whether you see external evidence immediately or not. When the prophets began prophesying in Ezra 5, they did not yet see all the glorious results we find in chapter 7. Instead the Jews and their leaders had to continue to work and contend with those trying to stop them. But the prophetic decree had gone forth and was working to shift the heavens and the earth.

Isaiah 55:11 declares, "So also will be the word that I speak; it does not return to me unfulfilled. My word performs my purpose and fulfills the mission I sent it out to accomplish"

(TPT). The declared word will continue working until it fulfills God's purpose.

To illustrate the force of the decreed word, allow me to relate the story of Hurricane Lili. Since we live in Florida, we stay aware of the weather conditions in the Gulf of Mexico, especially during hurricane season. One year a huge storm formed and developed into Hurricane Lili, which was heading directly toward the coast of Louisiana with wind speeds of 145 miles per hour. These wind speeds would leave catastrophic damage in their wake, so we were very concerned for friends of ours who lived in its path. As a matter of fact, I was supposed to travel to Louisiana on the Friday of that week to minister with these friends, but I realized that would not be possible if the hurricane hit on Thursday as predicted.

On Wednesday night, Larry Bizette, our friend and pastor of the church in Louisiana, called. I noticed his name on caller ID and told Tom that he must be calling to reschedule the time of ministry.

I answered the call, "Hello, Pastor Larry," to which he replied "Hello, Jane! We are all so excited about having you come minister for us this weekend."

Dismayed I said, "Pastor Larry, are you aware that a category four hurricane is supposed to hit your coast tomorrow morning?"

He replied, "Yeah, we know, but don't worry. We took care of Hurricane Lili."

So I said, "What do you mean you took care of Hurricane Lili?"

"Well," Larry explained, "remember how you came to our church last year and taught us about making decrees? After church tonight I gathered about twenty intercessors and we decreed, 'God, put Your finger in the eye of Hurricane Lili.' And we decreed that when the storm comes ashore tomorrow it will not be a category four storm with wind speeds of a hundred and forty-five miles per hour, but that it will be only a category one storm with wind speeds no greater than ninety miles per hour. So we took care of the storm. Looking forward to seeing you Friday!"

I wish I could tell you faith was rising in my heart, but sitting in my living room with me was my father, Frank Makosky, who was a retired meteorologist with the National Weather Service. I love watching the Weather Channel and have always been fascinated by hurricanes. So because of what I knew in my natural mind about hurricanes, I also knew that what Pastor Larry had decreed was impossible. Sometimes our natural knowledge interferes with our faith and can get us out of alignment with what God has decreed through the mouths of His prophetic people.

God taught me a big lesson that night. The next update on the Weather Channel described the catastrophic damage Hurricane Lili could do in Louisiana and urged people to prepare. It was a terrifying storm to watch. But then the meteorologist called attention to the eye of the storm, commenting that since the last update, for some unexplainable reason, the eye had begun to wobble and destabilize. There was nothing in their models to indicate a weakening of the storm, but, for some reason, the barometric pressure in the center of the storm, which had been dropping for 48 hours, had just taken a sudden turn upward.

If you are not familiar with the anatomy of a hurricane, allow me to explain. When the barometric pressure in the eye of the storm falls, the wind speeds go up. So in the same hour that Pastor Larry and his team made the decree "God, put Your finger in the eye of Hurricane Lili," the center or eye of the storm shifted! Over the next several hours the barometric pressure continued to climb, defying the scientific charts.

But here is where I understood the process of the decree. Five hours later, after continuous increase in barometric pressure, the wind speeds remained at the same powerful 145 miles per hour. So you see, when the decree was made it shifted something at the heart of the matter, yet on the outside it seemed nothing had changed.

Sometimes we make a decree and it seems nothing changes, but we must stay in faith, knowing the power of the word of the Lord, believing the heart of the matter has shifted.

The next morning Hurricane Lili hit the Louisiana coast. But it did not come ashore as a category four storm with 145-mile-an-hour winds. No, it came ashore as a category one storm with top winds of ninety miles an hour. On Friday when I arrived for the time of ministry, I knew that the Caribbean had suffered great damage, as had some parts of Louisiana, but this area of the decree was clearly not hard hit.

Pastor Larry showed me a copy of the newspaper with a headline that read, "God Puts His Finger in the Eye of Hurricane Lili." The decree saved the day.

## 7. Decrees Bring Things to Completion

Ezra wrote this regarding the completion of the Temple:

> And the elders of the Jews built and prospered through the prophesying of Haggai the prophet and Zechariah the son of Iddo. They finished their building by decree of the God of Israel and by decree of Cyrus and Darius and Artaxerxes king of Persia.
>
> Ezra 6:14 ESV

Prophesying, decreeing and building brought the project to completion.

The prophetic declarations over our lives and lands can go through a similar process as described in the book of Ezra. We receive the promise from the Lord by His decree, then the enemy comes along to discourage us and get us to stop by issuing a counter decree. God sends a prophetic word to revive vision and bring hope for fulfillment. We align with those purposes by reactivating the decree by our words. Then we see that God's original prophetic purpose is not just fulfilled but better than we ever hoped possible.

## YOUR DECLARATION

*I decree that I am in my Cyrus season. Things prophesied long ago are coming to pass. I have been released from captivity by the blood of Jesus; now I will arise and fulfill my calling as part of His Church, and the gates of hell will not prevail against me. I break out of every spirit of delay. I break off every spirit that would try to keep me silent. I am blessed and I have a voice. I break off every spirit that would try to spoil God's plans. When I declare the word of the Lord, it does not return to me unfulfilled but performs the purpose and fulfills the mission that it was sent to accomplish. God watches over His word to perform it. When I speak according to His will He watches over my words to perform them. I will declare a decree, then stay focused in faith as God brings it to pass.*

## YOUR ACTIVATION

Titus 2:15 says, "Declare these things; exhort and rebuke with all authority. Let no one disregard you." (ESV). The Greek word here for *authority* (*epitagēs*, *Strong's* 2003) means "command, order, an injunction by decree."

1. Identify promises you believe God has spoken over your life. Include any decrees given during prophecies or devotional times. Make a list of these decrees from the Lord.

2. Identify what the enemy might have spoken as a counter decree. Hint: If you are having a difficult time identifying what God has decreed, determine what you believe the enemy has decreed based on the challenges or struggles in your life. Then go back and complete point one, recognizing that the enemy's decree is the opposite of God's decree.

3. Write a declaration reaffirming and reactivating the decree of the Lord over your life. Include several Scriptures of support.

4. Identify both God's original decree and the enemy's counter decree over the place where you live. Write a decree that expresses God's intention for your territory.

# 3

# The Time of the Dynamo

"You shall receive power when the Holy Spirit has come upon you."

Acts 1:8

From the very beginning of God's interaction with mankind He has desired that His people, whom He created, hear His voice. Jesus said, "My sheep hear My voice" (John 10:27). This is for many reasons: fellowship, intimate heart-to-heart relationship with Him, fulfillment of Kingdom plans and divine purposes, strategies for advancement, strategies to defeat our enemies and that we might know God's times and seasons so we can position ourselves properly with prayers and decrees to cooperate with heaven.

This is why prophets, at different points of the year, press in to hear from heaven regarding the times and seasons we are entering, so our faith and expectation can be focused on accomplishing God's agenda.

During such a time, when I was praying and seeking the Lord regarding His times and seasons, I was awakened one morning by His voice saying, *You are coming into the time of the dynamo.* Being a person who loves words, I jumped up to study what the Lord was saying so I could work with heaven to see God's "dynamo" released in the earth.

## The Time of the Dynamo

I learned that a *dynamo* is a generator that produces direct current from which we get power and electricity.[1] But I wondered how this could possibly tie in to our spiritual experience for a new season. As I looked further, I discovered that the word *dynamo* comes from the same Greek word as *dunamis*, as do the words *dynamic* and *dynamite*. These are all strong words and are indicative of what God is preparing to do in the earth as His people are filled with Holy Spirit power.

*Dunamis* is found 119 times throughout the New Testament. Jesus used this word when He was preparing to ascend to heaven and be seated at the right hand of the Father. He gathered His disciples around Him and told them to return to Jerusalem and wait for the promise of the Father: "You shall receive power [*dunamis*] when the Holy Spirit has come upon you; and you shall be witnesses to Me in Jerusalem, and in all Judea and Samaria, and to the end of the earth" (Acts 1:8).

Jesus was speaking, of course, about the infilling of the Holy Spirit with the evidence of speaking in other tongues, as we see in Acts 2, which would empower the early Church to bring in a harvest of souls from the nations and change the world. Then, as now, the *dunamis*, or power, of the Holy Spirit within us works like a spiritual generator, releasing signs, wonders, miracles and a harvest of souls.

*Dunamis* is defined as the following: "force, might, strength, ability, miraculous power, abundance, the ability to perform miracles" (*Strong's* 1411). *Thayer's* lexicon gives us this additional definition: "an inherent power residing in a thing by virtue of its nature or which a person or thing exerts and puts forth; the power of performing miracles; power to achieve; the power and might of an army; moral power and excellence of soul; the power and influence which belongs to wealth and riches; power resting upon armies, forces and hosts."[2] Throughout Scripture we see the outpouring of the *dunamis* of the Holy Spirit generating miracles; revelation; faith; healing of hearts, minds and bodies; dreams, visions and prophecy; breakthrough; strength; and vitality.

All of this should be present in the life of a believer who has been filled with the Holy Spirit and is actively engaging in spiritual activities. Our prayers—whether praying "with my spirit" or "with my understanding" (1 Corinthians 14:15; see Jude 1:20)—act like a power generator that causes the impossible to become possible, the weak to become strong, the poor to become rich and activate angel armies to fight on our behalf. You can create an atmosphere of victory over your life by the words you speak with your mouth.

### Your Mouth Is a Generator

*Dunamis* is generated when we open our mouths and pray in our prayer languages. In his book *70 Reasons for Speaking in Tongues*, my father-in-law, Bishop Bill Hamon, expounds upon the divine power released when believers speak in the language of the Spirit.

More than 600 million Christians have received the gift of the Holy Spirit, yet most do not utilize this precious gift to its full potential. And many who do speak in tongues on a regular basis do not fully understand all the benefits this gift brings. . . . Our spirit language is the major key that unlocks the door to our spirit life and all of the attributes and manifestations of the Holy Spirit. The whole Christian life is lived and empowered by the Word of God and the Spirit of God.[3]

We must pursue the presence of God actively and passionately, stirring up the gift He has given us by opening our mouths and speaking in our Spirit languages. This generates untold power and unlocks every other blessing the Holy Spirit desires to give to us and to give through us.

What we say matters. The mouth is a generator. When used as the Holy Spirit purposes, it has the power to create—but remember that the tongue also has the power to destroy. We must stop cursing our situations with words of complaining, negativity and doubt. Why? Because these words become generators of things we do not want to be present in our lives. We can generate life or we can generate death. So stop cursing your ground! Stop speaking negative words against your body, your job, your family or your business. Faith-filled words create an atmosphere angels love to hang out in; words of negativity create an atmosphere inviting demonic spirits and oppression.

In a time of great contention and a war with words happening every day in the media and throughout the earth, we must live as those who speak life. This is a time of fresh commissioning for many who desire to see heaven invade earth.

## God Is Awakening a Force

For years our staff has begun each day by praying in tongues for an hour. Because I travel a lot, I am often not able to join them; however, one morning as I prayed with them I heard the Lord say, *I am awakening a force in the earth. Get ready! Get the people ready!* I felt a surge of excitement knowing this would be unlike anything we had ever experienced.

When we close out our prayer times we take a few minutes to share what each of us heard the Lord say. When I told what I had heard while in prayer, several of our younger staff members started laughing and whispering to one another.

Curious, I asked what I had said that was so funny. One of them explained that a new *Star Wars* movie was about to come out, and it was called *The Force Awakens*. I had not known that, and realized that God truly had a sense of humor in His timing of this word!

As I noted above, the word *force* is the first word used to describe the *dunamis* of God: "You shall receive power—*dunamis*, a force—when the Holy Ghost comes upon you." This force would have the potential to move immovable situations, to activate the miraculous and to work with supernatural strength and divine ability. This force, when released from our mouths, would have the power to break open the way where there seems to be no way. God was getting ready to awaken the force of the *dunamis* of the Holy Spirit within His people, and it would be generated through our mouths.

### Endunamao

A few weeks later I was praying in the Spirit and, honestly, was in a frustrating place in my life. I had been dealing with cycles of health issues; just when I thought I was over everything I would get sick again. It was not a serious sickness, but it left me exhausted and weak. My travel schedule allowed no spots where I could stay home to get caught up on rest, and that morning when I woke up I was unwell again.

As I prayed in the Spirit, I heard the Lord say to me over and over, *Be strong in the Lord and in the power of His might.* This verse, Ephesians 6:10, is a power-packed, force-filled Scripture. It brought life and strength to me that day and for the weeks to come. The word *power* in this verse is the Greek word *kratos,* which also means "force, strength, power and dominion" (*Strong's* 2904). The word *might* is the word *ischus* also means "force, forcefulness and strength" (*Strong's* 2479).

But the full revelation and impartation came to me when I studied the word *strong.* Rick Renner, in his book *Sparkling Gems from the Greek,* says this about *endunamao:*

> *Could you use some extra strength today?* I want to draw your attention to the word "strong" in Ephesians 6:10. It is the Greek word *endunamao,* a compound of the words *en* and *dunamis.* The word *en* means *in.* The word *dunamis* means *explosive strength, ability,* and *power.* It's where we get the word *dynamite.*
>
> Thus, this word *endunamao* presents the picture of an *explosive power that is being deposited into some type of container, vessel, or other form of receptacle.* The very nature of this word *endunamao* means that there necessarily must be some type of *receiver* for this power to be deposited *into.*
>
> *This is where we come into the picture!* We are specially designed by God to be the receptacles of divine power. When Paul tells us to be strong in the Lord, he is essentially saying, "Receive a supernatural, strengthening, internal deposit of power into your inner man." God is the Giver, and we are the *receptacles* into which this power is to be deposited.
>
> Paul knew you and I would desperately need supernatural power in order to successfully combat the attacks the enemy would bring against us.[4]

He goes on to explain that while making a historical study of how the Greeks used the word *endunamao,* he found further proof of the supernatural nature of the word. Classical Greeks used this word to refer to certain heroes, such as Hercules, who had been chosen by the gods and filled with supernatural power in order to accomplish supernatural assignments. I am in no way trying to endorse Greek mythology! This is merely an explanation of how the Greeks used this word and its application for us today. You see, you and I have been chosen by the true God and filled with His supernatural power to accomplish supernatural assignments in the earth. Everything we need in order to accomplish those assignments has been made available to us through the *dunamis* of the Holy Spirit within.

Wow! God was saying to me, *I want to fill you with My supernatural explosive power. I just need you to be a receptacle so you can receive. I will fill you with My divine enablement by filling you with My Spirit, and you will have supernatural power for your supernatural assignment.* Ephesians 6:10 came alive to me that day: "Be strong—be filled with explosive might and power—in the Lord and in the power of His might." That day was a turning point for me in my heart and in my health. Not only did I receive revelation, but I also received impartation from the Holy Spirit as I was filled with new strength and power.

## Your Mouth—The *Dynamo* Generator

Here are some things you generate when you open your mouth and speak, releasing the dynamo anointing—the *dunamis*, the power, of God.

### 1. Your Mouth Generates Miracle-Producing Power

As I mentioned, *dunamis* appears 119 times throughout the New Testament. While this word is translated a variety of ways, more than half the time it refers to a force for supernatural manifestations of healing, miracles and deliverance from evil spirits.

Jesus carried this power of God within Him continuously. When the woman pressed through the crowd to touch the hem of His garment, Jesus noticed. He commented that He felt virtue (*dunamis*) flow out of Him, which resulted in her healing. Every time Jesus opened His mouth to address a need, the sick were healed, the dead were raised, demons were cast out or storms were stilled. His mighty works amazed crowds and caused them to say among themselves, "What a word this is! For with authority and power He commands the unclean spirits, and they come out" (Luke 4:36). The *dunamis* of God is within us and is activated as we open our mouths to speak and decree. Miracles are generated by the words of our mouths.

A friend of mine once went to see a doctor about a problem with his knee. The diagnosis resulted in knee surgery. After the recovery period, however, his knee continued to give him trouble. The doctor told my friend that his knee would begin to improve if he would discipline himself daily to speak health and function to it, literally commanding the muscles and ligaments to be strengthened and restored. This doctor believed in the power of words to bring healing.

Initially my friend thought that advice was strange and not at all what he expected to hear from a well-known medical professional, but he ended up taking the words to heart. As a believer he decided to combine the doctor's advice with scriptural decrees. After a period of two months of decreeing healing to his knee every day, my friend told me that his knee was completely healed and restored.

I was once in a church service when the pastor called for anyone who was suffering from back problems to come forward for prayer. The altar area was filled quickly. I heard the Lord speak to me to ask the pastor if I could pray for certain

DECLARATIONS for BREAKTHROUGH

ones of those who had come forward. Rather than pray for healing, though, I felt the Lord impressing me to decree healing to those who could not bend their backs.

When I had obtained the pastor's permission and asked if anyone had this particular need, three people came to me—two older women and one six-foot-five man named Bill. Just as Peter and John told the lame man at the Beautiful Gate to look at them as they decreed healing to him, I asked each one to look me in the eye, and I boldly decreed healing to them.

Both of the elderly women had very limited movement in their backs, but after I decreed healing in the name of Jesus, both women received complete healing. Bill had no movement in his back at all. As I began to decree God's healing to him, I could see hopelessness in his eyes. So as I decreed I also began to prophesy, allowing the heart of the Lord to speak to the pain in not just his body but in his soul.

Then I paused and said, "Now begin to bend over as you receive your healing." You could see he had no faith to act on what I said; however, he began to bend, and continued to bend, until his hands went all the way to the floor. Afterward Bill told me that he had been in an accident more than a dozen years before and had had multiple surgeries, even one that fused the vertebrae in his back. Bending over was actually impossible! But after God healed him, full movement was completely restored.

Your mouth can generate your miracle.

### 2. Your Mouth Generates Prosperity-Producing Power

Scripture tells us that our mouths carry the power to generate provision, prosperity and success. The Lord spoke these words to Joshua:

> "This Book of the Law shall not depart from your mouth, but you shall meditate in it day and night, that you may observe to

do according to all that is written in it. For then you will make your way prosperous, and then you will have good success. Have I not commanded you? Be strong and of good courage; do not be afraid, nor be dismayed, for the LORD your God is with you wherever you go."

Joshua 1:8–9

Those within Hebraic culture who heard this understood the importance of not letting God's Word depart from their mouths. For most of us, the word *meditate* means pondering a Scripture or principle *internally*. But the Hebrew word is *hagah*, which means "to murmur, to ponder, to mutter, to speak, to talk, to utter, to study, to roar or to moan" (*Strong's* 1897).

In other words, we meditate when we speak the Word of God out loud, continually—not allowing it to depart from our mouths. Then, as we meditate on the Word, it strengthens our resolve to obey it; and our obedience leads in turn to the prosperity and success God desires us to have. This manner of decreeing the Scriptures, and also God's personal prophetic promises to us, creates an atmosphere for the blessings of the Lord to break open new opportunities.

One young couple in our church, Paul and Ashley Lackie, applied this principle of the decree to open the way financially for them to purchase a new home. At the time they had been married for ten years and had lived happily in a mobile home. But they knew God had told them it was time to purchase a home. Ashley explains:

We woke up Thursday morning and said, "Let's listen to our prophetic words and all the words from the Lord that have been released for this year." We discussed what we believed God had spoken to us and used that to write our decrees. We sat down and wrote out three pages of decrees, agreeing with the voice of God. We then took those decrees into the house we wanted, laid them on the counter, and prayed and decreed each one—and heaven responded. By Saturday morning we were under contract, and we were approved for the loan in fewer than twelve hours. We're so excited! It's a fulfillment of so many prophetic words. God put all the pieces together so easily and quickly. He was in every detail.

Your mouth can generate your breakthrough to make your way prosperous.

### 3. Your Mouth Generates Posterity-Producing Power

God loves to hear His words in the mouths of His people for another reason: The power that is generated can produce generational continuity and blessings. Isaiah 59:21 tells us:

> "As for Me," says the LORD, "this is My covenant with them: My Spirit who is upon you, and My words which I have put in your mouth, shall not depart from your mouth, nor from the mouth of your descendants, nor from the mouth of your descendants' descendants," says the LORD, "from this time and forevermore."

God wants to affirm His covenant by putting His words in our mouths to be shared from generation to generation.

There is a lot of teaching about generational curses; however, we can activate generational blessings as well by teaching children the Word of God and by training them to hear His voice.

A good example of this is prodigal children who return to the Lord in their adult lives because, suddenly, the words that they were taught by a godly adult came back to them and broke them free from bondage and rebellion. Whether it is for a person in your family or for someone else you love, it is never too late to activate the covenant of generational favor and blessings by making decrees before heaven.

A young man in his early twenties who was brought up by godly parents in our church ended up getting caught up in drugs and ran away from home. Months went by in which we did not know if he was alive or dead. One night during our Friday service, Tom began to decree and declare publicly the young man's name, saying, "Come home now! We call you out of wherever you are bound and declare you will come home now, in Jesus' name." His decree was both prophetic and intercessory in nature. The next morning the young man showed up on his parents' doorstep asking for help.

Your mouth is a force that generates freedom, deliverance and life.

### 4. Your Mouth Generates Peace-Producing Power

Have you ever been stressed by pressure, confusion or even chaos in your life or circumstances? Do you realize that God has given you power to create an atmosphere of peace through your words? If Jesus could speak to the winds and waves and say "Peace be still," and suddenly they were calmed, so, too, can we speak peace to tumultuous circumstances and see the peace of God prevail. Peace is a spiritual force that produces power to defeat the works of darkness: "The God of peace will soon crush Satan under your feet" (Romans 16:20 ESV). Our mouths can become the generators that shift an atmosphere from chaos into peace. (As a matter of fact, Hebrew scholars say the very letters used to form the word *shalom* convey the deeper meaning that peace comes when you destroy the authority of chaos.)

When challenges press in from every side we must be careful not to begin speaking negative, anxiety-filled words of worry, fear and doubt; rather, we must speak words of life. Proverbs 13:3 tells us that the one who keeps his tongue keeps his life. Proverbs 21:23 challenges us to "watch your words and be careful what you say, and you'll be surprised how few troubles you'll have" (TPT).

As I mentioned I travel a great deal for ministry, and there are times when packing a suitcase and leaving my family at home are difficult. But I have a decree I say out loud whenever I feel the pressure to become negative about my life. I say, "I love my life! I love my family. I love my husband. I love my call. I love the work of the Lord. I love the people I meet and the people I am blessed to minister to. I love the excitement of new places and new adventures. I was born for this. I am called to this. My family has grace for this. My marriage is stronger because we answer the call of God. My travel is a blessing not a curse. Thank You, Lord, for the honor to serve You in this way."

When I say this my whole attitude shifts; the atmosphere around my life becomes charged with positive, purposeful excitement to fulfill my next assignment. That peace becomes a force that causes the impossible to become possible.

Your mouth is a generator that can produce peace.

### 5. Your Mouth Generates God's Purposes

We must learn how to partner with God by the words we speak in order to co-labor with Him and help generate His divine purposes in the earth. The Lord challenged the prophet Isaiah with this mission: "I have put My words in your mouth; I have covered you with the shadow of My hand, that I may plant the heavens, lay the foundations of the earth, and say to Zion, 'You are My people'" (Isaiah 51:16). In other words, God put His words in Isaiah's mouth to "plant the heavens"—to effect change in the heavens—so that foundations could be laid in the earth, establishing Zion, His people, for the new day.

The word *plant* is the Hebrew word *nata*, which means "to strike in order to fix and establish, to fasten" (*Strong's*

5193). God was giving Isaiah the picture of an "open heaven," saying that He was anointing the words of the prophet to strike a blow in the heavenlies, which would form righteous foundations on the earth and establish God's rulership there.

In his book *Planting the Heavens*, Tim Sheets teaches us that our words are seeds and will produce after their kind.

> Words are seeds. "Word seeds" germinate and they grow. "Word seeds," planted properly, reproduce themselves. "Word seeds" are the concealed beginnings of something that can grow to fullness when we believe and act upon them. They are latent potential, waiting to be planted in the soil of an individual, a church, a business, or a nation that can grow and fulfill that "word seed."
>
> We are told that God planted the heavens and the earth with word seeds—words that became what He decreed. Heaven and earth became what He seeded, decreed, and described with His words. From the beginning God was sharing with man, who was made in His image and likeness, how they could partner with Him and be creators by decreeing word seeds. We do not create from nothing [as] God did, but we take what God has done and steward it in such a way that we can decree a creative force into the heavens and the earth. . . .
>
> We can plant words filled with life—words that when believed, decreed, and acted upon become the very thing they describe. . . .
>
> Plant words of life. Plant them in the heavens. Plant them on the earth. Plant them in your life, business, and children. Plant purpose-filled seeds.[5]

Our decrees have the power to shift the spiritual atmosphere over the earth that will in turn cause the earth to respond. Isaiah reflected upon this concept in this prophetic word: "Open up, O heavens, and pour out your righteousness. Let the earth open wide so salvation and righteousness can sprout up together. I, the LORD, created them" (Isaiah 45:8 NLT). We speak to the heavens and we declare to the earth, sowing word seeds that produce change.

One other aspect of planting the heavens with our decrees is that it causes angel armies to be activated to accomplish God's purpose. Psalm 103:20 says, "Bless the LORD, you His angels, who excel in strength, who do His word, heeding the voice of His word." Mighty angels in the heavenly realms are longing to be released on assignments to accomplish God's plans and purposes in the earth, but they are waiting. What are they waiting for? They are waiting to hear the voice or sound of His word. Yes, those words can come directly from God's throne in heaven; however, as His partners in the earth realm, we have been given access to hear His voice and release His words into the atmosphere, activating angels on earthly missions.

First Corinthians 13:1 tells us that when we speak in tongues, generating the *dunamis*, the power, of God, we might be speaking in an earthly human language we have not learned or we might be speaking in a heavenly angelic language. If you recall, one of the meanings of the word *dunamis* is "force"—a familiar military term, such as in the name *Air Force. Thayer's* lexicon says *dunamis* can be translated "the power that rests upon armies, forces or hosts" (*Strong's* 1411).

The angel armies, translated most often as "heavenly hosts," stand ready to hear God's commands, whether through the voice of God from heaven, the decreed word of the Lord from earth, or as they hear directives when God's people speak in tongues. What are they being sent to do? Angels are ministering spirits sent to assist those who are to inherit salvation (see Hebrews 1:14). That's us!

Your mouth can generate an open heaven and mobilize angel armies.

## YOUR DECLARATION

*I am a dynamo, a powerhouse for God's glory, generating light to light up my world. My words will change my world because the dynamo, the power, is in my mouth. I am a power producer! My mouth will generate miracles. My mouth will generate freedom. My mouth will generate breakthrough in my life and the lives of others. My mouth will activate angel armies.*

## YOUR ACTIVATION

1. Choose an area in your life in which you need to see breakthrough. Begin to pray fervently in the Spirit, generating an atmosphere of freedom. Take time to listen to the Holy Spirit and write down what He decrees over you.

2. Choose one of the above areas (miracles, prosperity, posterity, peace, God's purposes) and prayerfully write a decree to generate power in that area of your life.

# Activating the Dynamo Anointing

By your decree everything stands at attention, for all that you have made serves you.

Psalm 119:91 TPT

While Jesus was on the earth, He demonstrated breakthrough in every realm and in everything He did. He demonstrated breakthrough over sickness and disease as He healed many and did mighty miracles. He demonstrated breakthrough over poverty as He multiplied five loaves and two fish and fed a multitude of five thousand. He sent His friend to catch a fish with a coin in its mouth to pay certain taxes. He demonstrated breakthrough over oppression and prejudice as He spoke with the Samaritan and Syrophoenician women, and gave Mary permission to sit and learn spiritual things, even though it was forbidden for women to do so. He demonstrated breakthrough over nature as He decreed, "Peace, be still!" and the wind and waves obeyed Him. Jesus demonstrated breakthrough over the human religious systems, for they were a substitute for the reality of relationship with the living God. Ultimately, He demonstrated breakthrough over death, hell and the grave.

In the midst of these demonstrations of breakthrough, He said something so fantastic that two thousand years later we are still trying to grasp the fullness of His words. He said this: "He who believes in Me, the works that I do, he will do also; and greater works than these he will do; because I go to the Father" (John 14:12 NASB). Jesus was saying we would carry the same anointing for breakthrough in every realm and in all we do because He was going to the Father. He told His disciples, "Here's the truth: It's to your advantage that I go away, for if I don't go away the Divine Encourager will not be released to you. But after I depart, I will send him to you" (John 16:7 TPT). He knew the disciples were going to need the power of the Holy Spirit in order to turn the world upside down. He encouraged them that while He was on earth He could walk with them, but when the Father sent the Holy Spirit, He would not just be with them; He would be in them (see John 14:16–18).

So, when the Holy Spirit comes to live in us, His power is a dynamo, a generator enabling supernatural abilities with every breath. Now it is simply up to us to activate every anointing the Holy Spirit has made available to us through His constant presence in our lives. As we understand the full intention of the *dunamis* of God, the power that is resident in us, we also gain greater ability to recognize His voice and greater clarity to make decrees.

Here are a few words of dynamo anointing for us to activate in order to hear the word of the Lord and bring breakthrough to our world.

## 1. The Anointing for Superhuman Energy

*Webster's* defines the word *dynamo* in two ways. The first, which was mentioned in the previous chapter, is a power generator. The second is a forceful, energetic individual. We might call this person a "fireball" or a "live wire." It brings to mind someone who is full of life, full of energy, a larger than life personality. People who are dynamos are forces to be reckoned with. Remember, the first definition of *dunamis* was the word *force*. You are a force to be reckoned with! His Church is a force to be reckoned with!

Such is the anointing God desires to stir up within His people when we pray in the power of the Holy Spirit. James 5:16 says that "the effective, fervent prayer of a righteous man avails much." The word *fervent* is the Greek word *energeo*, which means "to be active, efficient, operative, to activate, to energize, divine energy put forth to effectually bring forth tangible, noticeable change" (*Strong's* 1754).

*Energeo* acts like a key turning in the ignition of a car. All the horsepower is at rest within the engine until the key turns it on. What is the key? It is the Word and Spirit of God. What is the ignition? It is your mouth. When we ignite the power of the Holy Spirit through speaking and decreeing and praying in the Holy Ghost, explosive strength and *dunamis* are released. This fountain of energy can change your body, soul and spirit, and release God's miracle power in you and through you.

## YOUR DECLARATION

*Because the Holy Spirit lives in me, I am filled with superhuman energy and strength. My body is strong, my eyes are open, my mind is sharp and my spirit is ready to step through every door of favor and influence God opens for me. I will activate my spirit language and ignite the fire of God within me as I open my mouth to pray and decree. I am a force to be reckoned with. I am a dynamo. I am a fireball, a generator of miracles. I will run and not be weary; I will walk and not faint. I am fully energized to accomplish my calling. I will not just survive, but I will thrive because God's Holy Spirit dynamo in me is generating supernatural strength.*

As we make this decree, I hear God declaring these words:

## THE LORD DECREES

*"Supernatural energy will surge into believers who have embraced their missions. I will energize them for service and activate My power within to break weariness, heaviness, fear, discouragement and defeat. I decree that new hope and joy will surge in the souls of the Kingdom-minded, enabling an expansion of influence, favor and divine connection.*

*"I, the Lord, am filling you full of energy, passion and zeal. You will be anointed with supernatural strength to accomplish every assignment in My name."*

What a promise! So right now, pray in the Holy Ghost, then breathe in God's life, health, strength and vitality. Allow your body, mind, heart and spirit to receive new strength, now in

Jesus' name. Receive His supernatural energy that comes by being filled with the Holy Spirit of God.

## 2. The Anointing for Harvest

Remember these words that Jesus told His disciples: "You will receive power when the Holy Spirit has come upon you; and you shall be My witnesses both in Jerusalem and in all Judea, and Samaria, and as far as the remotest part of the earth" (Acts 1:8 NASB). Jesus knew that His Church would need empowerment from the Holy Spirit in order to change the world and bring in the massive harvest. They could not accomplish it in their own strength. But by His explosive power released through the lives of His disciples, individuals, cities and even nations could be changed.

The word *dynamite* comes from the same root word as *dunamis* and is a picture of this explosive power God has put within us. Just as dynamite is used to blow up a mountainside to create a new roadway, so, too, the *dunamis* of the Holy Spirit blows up the resistance of sin, pride, religion, idolatry and unbelief to establish a new path forward. Revival comes as God's *dunamis* is demonstrated. The apostle Paul spoke of this power when he told the church at Corinth, "My speech and my preaching was not with enticing words of man's wisdom, but in demonstration of the Spirit and of power [*dunamis*]" (1 Corinthians 2:4 KJV). To the believers in Rome he said that the Gospel is the "power [*dunamis*] of God unto salvation" (Romans 1:16 KJV).

Sharing the Gospel, demonstrating a miracle or ministering a prophetic word to an unbeliever carries the explosive *dunamis* of God to deliver that person out of the kingdom of darkness.

I once shared a prophetic word with a man while on a flight coming home from a ministry trip in Buffalo, New York. It was apparent when he sat down that he had had too much to drink. He kept trying to engage me in conversation, and I kept giving him monosyllabic answers indicating I did not really want to talk to him. Then I heard the Lord say to put my magazine down and talk to the man.

As we began to chat he asked me what I do for a living. I said, "I am a minister."

Suddenly the man's whole demeanor changed. He was instantly transformed from a friendly drunk into a seething, angry man. "A minister? A minister?" And he began to yell and unleash a tirade of profanity against me.

I sat there thinking, *Lord, You told me to talk to him!* Immediately I knew that God wanted me to minister to this man, so while he was cursing me, I activated the *dunamis* of the Holy Spirit within me and listened for His voice.

As the man began to wind down, I said simply, "Thank you for sharing your heart." (I mean, really, what else can you say while being cussed out and preparing to minister a prophetic word?) I went on to say, "But as you were 'sharing' I heard God tell me how much He loves you and understands your anger since you were so mistreated by a priest when you were a boy. That wasn't His heart for you at all!"

The man sobered up instantly and stared at me silently with his mouth open.

I went on, "And He wants you to know that the child you have lost to some religious cult is going to be okay and is going to come home. He loves you and wants you to know He will do this for you."

The man who only minutes before was yelling and cursing me, suddenly put his hands over his face and began to weep.

He was shaking his head and saying, "No God that I have ever heard of loves me."

To which I replied, "Then you might not know the real God, because He really does love you."

The man wiped the tears from his face, turned to me and said, "Why don't you tell me about Him then," and for the next two hours I shared the truth of the Gospel with this man. When our flight landed, he allowed me to pray with him. The *dunamis* of God released through a prophetic word and Scripture unlocked this man's life and brought healing to his broken heart.

### Your Declaration

*I am filled with power to be a witness for Christ. The dynamo in me will generate light to light up my world. I will be bold and courageous and will operate in the gifts of the Spirit to bring in the harvest of souls. I am a soul winner. I am a nation-changer and will stand my ground under pressure. My words will release revival. My words will shift the atmosphere because the dynamo is in my mouth. Miracles are in my mouth. Prophetic words are in my mouth. Deliverance and healing are in my mouth. I will speak with authority and demons will flee, angels will be loosed and the Kingdom of God will advance. I decree this in Jesus' name.*

### The Lord Decrees

*"You have entered a time of amped-up, dynamic 'power encounters' as you pray in the Spirit, acting as a human dynamo, a generator of God's presence, power and potential, which will result in a mighty harvest of souls for*

*My Kingdom. I will strip away every religious pretense and begin to reveal My true nature and inherent power within My Church to transform the world that I so love. My voice from your mouth will shake the heavens and the earth, and My power and authority will be released through the voice of My Bride, the Church, who is arising with new grace and beauty and demonstrating My Kingdom with unrivaled authority. Her purity and regal nature, displayed through My people, will silence those who have sought to mock and scorn her.*

*"As a matter of fact, salvation will spring up from some of the most unlikely places as I turn Sauls into Pauls. The persecutors will become My propagators. The mockers will become My mouthpieces. The hostile will become My heroes. The places of great contending will become My place of great harvest," says the Lord. "Watch what I will do through My power to save, for I will astound even you," says the Lord.*

*"In the midst of great chaos and contention in the earth, you will face darkness and persecution, but My glory will rise on you. Resist the forces of resistance and they will flee from you. Decide now not to bend your knee to the pressure to conform to this world. It's time for awakening and revival, which will come by My power. My Spirit in you will cause this to be your finest hour!"*

## 3. The Anointing to Break through Impossibility

Jesus said, "If you can believe, all things are possible to him who believes." (Mark 9:23). In this passage we have another dimension of the dynamo anointing. The word *possible* is the Greek *dunata*, which comes from the same root word as *dunamis*. *Dunata* speaks of one's capabilities, meaning "powerful, able, possible, capable, strong, full of potential" (*Strong's* 1415). *Dunata* is the ability to function as one who is mission-minded, one who views the world through the lens of possibilities. The one who has the Holy Spirit dynamo within has the ability to dream big dreams and then turn them into missions, turning dreams into reality.

There is a truth that illustrates what I call "the principle of the 'one-man' breakthrough." It is this: When one person breaks through a barrier in a specific area, it opens the way for others to break through in the future.

We saw this with athletes trying to break the four-minute mile. Prior to May 6, 1954, skeptics purported that it was physically impossible for the human body to achieve this goal. A young British athlete named Roger Bannister, however, set his eyes on the prize, made it his mission in life to be the first, and one day turned his dream into a reality: He ran a mile in 3 minutes and 59.4 seconds. Once he broke through that barrier, more than fourteen hundred people have since accomplished the same. One person broke through, so many could break through.

In another instance, on October 12, 2019, a Kenyan long-distance runner named Eliud Kipchoge ran a marathon, 26.2 miles, in 1 hour, 59 minutes and 40 seconds—the first person in recorded history to break the two-hour barrier, another feat previously thought impossible.

On that day he said, "I can tell people that no human is limited. I expect more people all over the world to run under two hours after today."[1] He was saying that what was once thought to be impossible had now been made possible because one individual broke through.

With this understanding we can define the word *impossible* as "that which absolutely, positively cannot be done . . . until somebody does it!"

This is a time when God wants to challenge His people regarding our mindsets of impossibilities. He wants us to believe that when we activate our faith, all things are possible. When we pray in our spirit language, believing that we are dynamos, our faith gets released to a new level to face impossibilities (see Jude 1:20). The *dunamis* of the Holy Spirit within us causes us to live in an atmosphere of unlimited potential; anything becomes possible.

## YOUR DECLARATION

*Because I am a Holy Spirit dynamo, I will dream impossible dreams. I will do impossible things and accomplish my life's mission. I will reach and then exceed my potential. I am a one-person breakthrough. I am not a victim; I am a victor. I will break through so others can break through. I am able, capable and competent for any task. I am strong in faith, courage and power. I live in an atmosphere of unlimited potential where anything is possible.*

## THE LORD DECREES

*"I am expanding your assignments and accelerating your timeline. I will take you from 'mission impossible' to 'mission accomplished.' I will shift vision into mission, as I have made you supernaturally capable and well able to face the giants. You will experience My nature as the Breaker and will see every challenge as an opportunity for victory. As the Church generates power through her prayers, I will cause breakthrough to come on a national level in many lands. I will anoint some to be dynamos in government to confront the evil ones*

*who are on a mission to hijack the destiny of nations.*
*As a new prayer movement arises, the spirit prayers*
*will generate power and light that will shine in places*
*of darkness and corruption and bring exposure. Rise up*
*and break through and advance My Kingdom cause."*

## 4. The Anointing for "Crazy Increase"

I had a dream in which God challenged me to believe for "crazy increase." In the dream I saw the rapid multiplication of the cells of a baby being formed in the womb. I also saw the process of a seed growing into a tree and producing fruit with hundreds, even thousands of seeds. That is "crazy increase."

The dream went on, and I began to see the scene from Genesis 26 in which, although there was famine in the land, Isaac was told by the Lord to stay and sow seed. "Isaac sowed in that land, and reaped in the same year a hundredfold; and the LORD blessed him. The man began to prosper, and continued prospering until he became very prosperous" (Genesis 26:12–13). In the dream the Lord said, *That is the one-hundredfold anointing of "crazy increase."*

When I awoke from the dream, I began to study the concept of reaping one-hundredfold. I had previously thought this meant one hundred times; however, the Jewish people used it to denote blessings without measure.

Think of this illustration. If you were to take a piece of paper and fold it in half, you would then have two sections. If you folded it a second time, you would have four sections. If you folded it a third time you would have sixteen sections, and on and on. If you were able to continue folding the page thirty, sixty and even one hundred times, you would end up with numbers so large I had to look up the value. Thirty folds would produce 1,073,701,824 (that's one billion, seventy-three million, seven hundred and one thousand, eight hundred and twenty-four) sections. Sixty folds would yield 1,151,973,021,073,889,216 (that's one quintillion, one hundred fifty-one quadrillion, nine hundred seventy-three trillion, twenty-one billion, seventy-three million, eight hundred eighty-nine thousand, two hundred sixteen) sections. Finally, if you were able to fold the page one hundred times you would end up with 1,201,064,595,207,167,685,882,431, 343,616 (that's one nonillion, two hundred and one octillion, sixty-four septillion, five hundred ninety-five sextillion, two hundred seven quintillion, one hundred sixty-seven quadrillion, six hundred eighty-five trillion, eight hundred eighty-two billion, four hundred thirty one million, three hundred forty-three thousand, six hundred-sixteen) sections.[2] Now that is "crazy increase"!

So what does this have to do with the dynamo anointing? Look at this Scripture: "God is able to make all grace abound toward you, that you, always having all sufficiency in all things, may have an abundance for every good work" (2 Corinthians 9:8). The word *able* is the Greek word *dunatos*, which is from the same root word as *dunamis*, but this word addresses the concept of wealth and influence. *Thayer's* lexicon gives this as one of the definitions for *dunamis*: "the power and influence which belongs to wealth and riches" (*Thayer's* 1411). And it gives this for *dunatos*: "mighty in wealth and influence" (*Thayer's* 1415). The word *abound* in this verse means "to superabound and be in excess, abundance and increase" (*Strong's* 4053).

I love the wording of this verse in the Passion Translation: "Yes, God is more than ready to overwhelm you with every form of grace, so that you will have more than enough of everything—every moment and in every way. He will make you overflow with abundance in every good thing you do."

So this time of supernatural, superabundant blessing causes an internal dynamo anointing and generates wealth, favor and influence for your Kingdom assignment. In the words of Psalm 115:14, "May the LORD increase you more and more." It is time to stir up the anointing from the Lord, who is able to bring you into "crazy increase."

## YOUR DECLARATION

*I am living in "crazy increase"! I will have more than enough to supply my needs and to accomplish my mission. God will bless me so I can be a blessing. All that the enemy has stolen must be restored seven times. I am a tither and a giver, so this is my time. I am a one-hundredfold believer and a one-hundredfold receiver. Every seed I plant will superabound with increase. I have more than enough of everything—every moment and in every way—and will overflow with abundance in every good thing I do.*

## THE LORD DECREES

*"It's time for 'crazy increase.' I am dealing ruthlessly with the spirits of lack, limitation and robbery, which have kept My people down. As you give cheerfully I will cause you to superabound and excel, to increase and overflow and to experience more than enough. I will take you out of 'not enough' or 'barely enough' into a time of more than enough. You will have what you need to live, grow, accomplish your mission and be abundantly blessed. You will begin prospering and continue prospering until you become very prosperous."*

## 5. The Anointing to Prophesy

Prophets are God's mouthpieces for the earth. We have noted the words of the prophet Amos, that God will do nothing unless He first reveals His secrets to His servants the prophets (see Amos 3:7), and of the prophet Isaiah, that the voice of the Lord will shatter our enemies (see Isaiah 30:31). And recall that God told the prophet Jeremiah, "I have put My words in your mouth . . . to root out and to pull down, to destroy and to throw down, to build and to plant" (Jeremiah 1:9–10). God wants to put His words in our mouths.

Recall that on the Day of Pentecost the Holy Spirit was poured out on the believers gathered in the Upper Room, filling them with the *dunamis*, the power, of God. As they spilled out of the room and began to preach the Gospel in the streets of Jerusalem in new tongues, Peter stood up and began to quote a Scripture from the prophet Joel: "And it shall come to pass in the last days, says God, that I will pour out of My Spirit on all flesh; your sons and your daughters shall prophesy, your young men shall see visions, your old men shall dream dreams" (Acts 2:17). The *dunamis* of God in the life of every Spirit-filled believer will cause prophetic revelation to be released in and through our lives.

Second Chronicles 20:20 declares this: "Believe in the LORD your God, and you shall be established; believe His prophets, and you shall prosper." The word *prosper* in Hebrew means "to move forward, advance, to break out, to break through, to become a success, to become profitable, to become prosperous" (*tsalach*, *Strong's* 6743). If you have ever felt stuck in this past season, you can enter into grace for acceleration of purpose as you believe and speak the prophetic voice of God. We are coming into unprecedented times of advancement for God's Kingdom purposes.

There is a new generation of prophets and prophetic people who will release the voice of God and who will also demonstrate Kingdom transformation in cities and nations. Signs and wonders will become more in evidence as we demonstrate the reality of who God is by speaking with the *dunamis* of the Spirit until we see things shift.

It is time to prophesy and decree by the Spirit of the living God. It is time for a great harvest. It is time to see the Gospel of Christ become the power of God unto salvation. It is time to activate our faith and generate signs, wonders and miracles by the dynamo anointing within.

─────────── YOUR DECLARATION ───────────

*God has put His words in my mouth, so I will prophesy over my life, my home, my family, my city and my nation. I will war with the prophecies that have gone before me. My mouth will be used as the sword of the Lord to declare His justice in the earth. The voice of the Lord in my mouth will shatter the enemy. As I believe what God says, I will prosper, move forward, advance, break out, break through and become a success. I will be God's voice to my generation.*

─────────── THE LORD DECREES ───────────

*"Where are My Elijahs? Where are My Elishas? Where are the Deborahs and the Daniels? For My Holy Spirit dynamo has been activated, and I am generating dreams, visions and prophecies for My people to declare. I am anointing you like Jeremiah of old, and I am putting My words in your mouth. You will prophesy to root out false ideologies, to pull down illegitimate structures, to*

*throw down the enemy's lies and to destroy the king-
dom of darkness. Then you will be one of those who
will build and plant My Kingdom in the midst of the
earth. You will be My Kingdom ambassador with My
decrees on your lips. You will open the heavens with
your words and bring heaven down to earth to manifest
My will. Rise up! Speak with boldness, for I will have a
prophetic company and this will be their finest hour."*

## 6. The Anointing for Extraordinary Miracles

The power of God produces miracles. Scripture tells us, for
instance, that "God kept releasing a flow of extraordinary
miracles through the hands of Paul" (Acts 19:11 TPT). The
word *extraordinary* is *tynchano*, and it refers to miracles that
"hit the mark, that are mighty, exceptional or out of the ordinary deeds" (*Strong's* 5177). These are miracles we reach for;
it speaks of anointing we become masters of. Because Paul
had the dynamo of the Holy Spirit within, these extraordinary
miracles could happen continually as long as he was generating them by his faith.

*Thayer's* lexicon describes *dunamis* as "the power for performing miracles" (*Thayer's* 1411). Every believer can operate
in miracles. You might think that is not your allotment from
the list of spiritual gifts; however, remember that Mark 9:23
challenges us with Jesus' words: "All things are possible to
him who believes." Remember, the Greek word for *possible*
is *dunata*, which means "one who is capable, able or competent," also from the same root word as *dunamis*.

How are all things, even miracles, made possible? We must
believe. The Greek word for *believe* in this verse comes from
the root word *pistis*, which means "to be actively reaching
forward to grab hold of something." It means "activated faith"

(*Strong's* 4102). So when we reach forward and grab hold of a miracle, for ourselves or another, we are made able to generate supernatural power and all things become possible. Our miracles will hit the mark every time.

Jesus challenges believers this way:

> "These signs will follow those who believe: In My name they will cast out demons; they will speak with new tongues; they will take up serpents; and if they drink anything deadly, it will by no means hurt them; they will lay hands on the sick, and they will recover."
>
> Mark 16:17–18

It says these signs will follow believers—not just pastors, prophets or evangelists. Every believer can activate and generate the supernatural power of God by speaking and decreeing God's word.

———— YOUR DECLARATION ————

*Because I am a believer, signs will follow me in all I do. I grab hold of miracles and release miracles to others. I am a miracle worker. My hands were made to be laid on the sick so that they will recover. My words will generate supernatural power that will flow from me continuously to set captives free, to reverse the curse and even to raise the dead. Because I believe, nothing is impossible for me. I will generate miracles that hit the mark every time. I decree this in Jesus' name.*

———— THE LORD DECREES ————

*"Now is the time for miracles, signs and wonders that will hit the mark and get the attention of unbelievers*

*worldwide. You will be My carrier of power, My dy-
namo, who will break the yoke of infirmity, sickness,
deterioration, disease and death. Prepare to be surprised
at all I do through you, for even as you begin to speak,
I will already have answered by power. Even now, receive the* dunamis *that will heal you, strengthen you
and set you free."*

## 7. The Anointing for Excellence of Soul

When a believer is filled with the *dunamis* of God, not only
does he or she receive the power to perform miracles, to
prophesy, to break through impossibility, to unlock "crazy
increase" or to have supernatural energy to bring in a harvest
of souls, but he or she also receives an anointing for inner
transformation.

The apostle Paul prophesied to the people of Corinth what
was on God's heart by sharing these words that the Lord had
spoken to him: "My grace is sufficient for you, for My strength
is made perfect in weakness" (2 Corinthians 12:9). The word
for *strength* is *dunamis*, "having moral power and excellence
of soul" (*Thayer's* 1411). This word is used to describe a force
or power that produces the necessary ability to make needed
changes. It is the inner strength to face personal challenges
and to overcome.

I experienced this power as a teenager who had recently
been filled with the Holy Spirit. I had my first taste of *dunamis* that transformed my soul. As a child I had suffered abuse
from a neighbor and had never told my parents about it. As a
matter of fact I pushed the memories and trauma down deep
into my soul. But after I was saved and later filled with the
Holy Spirit, all those memories began coming to the surface.
God wanted to heal me in the deepest place of my heart.

DECLARATIONS for BREAKTHROUGH

One night, overwhelmed by the shame and pain, I went into my bedroom and got down on my knees, praying in the Spirit with tears, groaning and travail. The flood of my spirit language poured out of me as a river of living water as the Holy Spirit interceded through me for me. It was one of the most intense experiences of my life. After an hour or more of this encounter, my tongues changed to English, and I began interceding for my abuser, forgiving him and praying for his salvation. Only the Holy Spirit can do such a quick and deep work. When I got off my knees I was lighter and freer, and from that time until now I have been completely healed of the trauma.

Romans 8:26 explains what happened to me that night: "Likewise the Spirit also helps in our weaknesses. For we do not know what we should pray for as we ought, but the Spirit Himself makes intercession for us with groanings which cannot be uttered." The Holy Spirit's intercession was a dynamo anointing within me, generating healing, freedom and life.

Dealing with weakness is never fun. But the apostle Paul had a whole different perspective on it.

> But [the Lord] answered me, "My grace is always more than enough for you, and my power finds its full expression through your weakness." So I will celebrate my weaknesses, for when I'm weak I sense more deeply the mighty power of Christ living in me. So I'm not defeated by my weakness, but delighted! For when I feel my weakness and endure mistreatment—when I'm surrounded with troubles on every side and face persecution because of my love for Christ—I am made yet stronger. For my weakness becomes a portal to God's power.
>
> 2 Corinthians 12:9–10 TPT

Wow! "My weakness becomes a portal to God's power." That is transformative. It is what Joel said regarding preparation for a time of war: "Let the weak say, 'I am strong'" (Joel 3:10). This could also be translated, "Let the weak say, 'I am a warrior; I am a champion'" (see *Strong's* 1368). When God's strength comes, it turns everything around.

---

## YOUR DECLARATION

*I am a warrior. I am a champion. God's Spirit is a dynamo in me, generating power to heal my soul. When faced with personal challenges or weaknesses, I am an overcomer by God's grace. I bring my pain or trauma to Jesus. If I am persecuted or mistreated I will rejoice, since I am not defeated but victorious. His Spirit has an answer for whatever I need. When I am weak God floods me with supernatural strength. When I am hurt He touches and heals my heart. When I am sad He brings me joy. My weakness is a portal to God's power. His grace is more than enough for me.*

---

## THE LORD DECREES

*"Now receive My supernatural enablement to lift you out of your pain, hurt and distress. I have not left you, nor forsaken you. I live in you every moment of every day. My Holy Spirit dwells in you whether you feel strong or weak. Allow Me to set you free from your past and liberate your soul to be mighty for Me. You are a warrior! I am breaking the chains of abuse, rejection, abandonment, fear and pain. You are free because My Spirit dwells in you. Stir up My Spirit. Activate My healing power. I stand ready to heal you and deliver you, and to do even more. I will make you a healer and a deliverer, freeing a generation of its sorrows,*

*disappointments and shame. You are a new creation in Christ Jesus, full of power, full of peace and full of joy in the Holy Ghost."*

 YOUR ACTIVATION

Take the time to go back through this chapter and read the declarations and God's decrees. Then write in a journal any additional personalized decrees He speaks to you in each area. Receive the Holy Spirit's anointing to generate what you lack. Remember, any area of weakness becomes a portal to His power!

# The Breaker Is Here

The breaker is come up before them.

Micah 2:13 KJV

When God speaks, things change. When we agree with what God speaks, we are changed. Yes, my friend, one word from God will change everything.

Part of the purpose of this book is to share prophetic words God has spoken to me through the years. Though these words were spoken to me at different times and in different seasons, I think you will find that each of these decrees is timeless. Each one powerfully highlights truth from the Scriptures and can, therefore, be taken as a living promise to be confessed and decreed. Each decree from the throne of God serves to connect our hearts to the One who loves us and desires to see us break through every challenge. The voice of the Lord always brings breakthrough when we stir up our faith and agree with it.

## The Breaker Is Here

As I walked into church one Sunday morning, I heard the Lord say, *Tell them, "The Breaker is here."* Yes, I knew He meant "here" at our church, but He was also announcing He is "here" in this season to bring breakthrough for His people. Micah 2:13 (AMPC) says, "The Breaker [the Messiah] will go up before them. They will break through, pass in through the gate and go out through it, and their King will pass on before them, the Lord at their head."

The Message translation says it this way: "Then I, GOD, will burst all confinements and lead them out into the open. They'll follow their King. I will be out in front leading them."

The Word *breaker* in Hebrew is *parats*, which means "to break out, to burst forth, compel, to urge, grow, increase, open, to break in pieces, to break up, to break open, to break out (violently), to break off all limitation" (*Strong's* 6555).

Wow! Jesus, our Breaker, is here to burst through all confinements and break us out of all limitations. Limitations on finances? Limitations on health? Limitations on emotional health and well-being? Jesus has come to break into pieces all constrictions and to cause us instead to burst forth. This is what He died for—to break us out of the constriction and bondage of sin, sickness and separation from God. He longs to make us truly free.

When limitations are broken, all unhealthy patterns from the past are shattered. Now you can grow. Now you can increase. Now you can succeed. Your mind can be renewed to think as the Breaker (Jesus) thinks. Nothing is impossible. This Breaker anointing is not just for personal freedom though. It creates vision and forward momentum for the Kingdom to advance.

In Scripture we see that Jesus, the disciples and the early Church all understood the power of decreeing what God was saying or what they understood He wanted to do in the moment. It was not enough simply to hear the voice of God or sense His intended desires; they teach us that the voice of the Lord must be declared. Why? Because God wants to bring breakthrough to people over every force of darkness and victory in every circumstance—and breakthrough always has a sound.

Consider the example of Joshua and the walls of Jericho. God had given Joshua the declaration by which Israel would bring down the massive walls of the city (see Joshua 6). But it was not until the prescribed time when the trumpets blew and the army shouted with a great shout that heaven was activated to cause the walls to crumble supernaturally. Throughout Scripture, by the way, the trumpet is used as a symbol of the prophetic voice of the Lord (see Numbers 10:1–10; Revelation 1:10). As the trumpets blew around Jericho, the word of the Lord was being declared. As the people shouted, faith began to arise, stirring heaven to fight for Israel and do for them that which they could not do for themselves. Breakthrough has a sound.

## A New Sound

Another interesting and pertinent aspect of the sound of breakthrough is that the word for *great shout* is the Hebrew word *t'ruwah*, which is also the word *jubilee*, a time of celebration, a time of freedom from debt and a time for reconnecting to one's inheritance. *T'ruwah* means an acclamation of joy, a battle cry, to blow the trumpets, to sound an alarm, a great shout, a shout of victory, rejoicing (*Strong's* 8643). It comes from the root word *ruwa*, which means "to mar by breaking, to split the ears with sound, to rejoice, to destroy, a sound of triumph, a joyful sound, to sound an alarm" (*Strong's* 7321). God's jubilee sound in heaven is declaring release, but God is also listening for the sound of jubilee coming from His people in the earth. An alarm, a war cry, is reverberating in heaven, and God desires to hear a corresponding sound of urgency and fervency from His people.

Can we release both the sound of rejoicing in victory and the war cry of battle? When the sounds of heaven and earth connect, a resonating battle cry will go out for God's angel armies to bring breakthrough for us as never before. The jubilee shout at Jericho caused walls to fall!

Gideon had been given the word of the Lord and the prophetic strategy of heaven to defeat Israel's oppressive enemies (see Judges 7:1–23). God's people were dramatically outnumbered, tens of thousands against a mere three hundred. But Gideon instructed the army to surround the enemy's camp when it was dark and make a sound. In unison they smashed the pitchers that contained lamps, and simultaneously blew the trumpets. The Israelites had a torch in one hand, a trumpet in the other hand and the word of the Lord in their mouths declaring, "The sword of the LORD and of Gideon!" The magnified sound of this unseen army of Israel terrified their enemy and caused them to flee. God's people overcame their enemy against incredible odds because breakthrough has a sound.

At another time, when Judah was surrounded by enemy nations, King Jehoshaphat called for the people to fast and pray. In the midst of this solemn assembly, Jahaziel arose and spoke a prophetic word regarding the victory that was to come.

And he said, "Listen, all you of Judah and you inhabitants of Jerusalem, and you, King Jehoshaphat! Thus says the LORD to you: 'Do not be afraid nor dismayed because of this great multitude, for the battle is not yours, but God's. Tomorrow go down against them. They will surely come up by the Ascent of Ziz, and you will find them at the end of the brook before the Wilderness of Jeruel. You will not need to fight in this battle. Position yourselves, stand still and see the salvation of the LORD, who is with you, O Judah and Jerusalem!' Do not fear or be dismayed; tomorrow go out against them, for the LORD is with you."

2 Chronicles 20:15–17

In response Jehoshaphat encouraged the people with this declaration: "Believe in the LORD your God, and you shall be established; believe His prophets, and you shall prosper" (verse 20). Remember, the word for *prosper* is the Hebrew word *tsalach*, which means to push forward, to advance, to break out, to succeed, to prosper and to become profitable (*Strong's* 6743). The prophetic word always goes before us and causes breakthrough, advancement and blessing.

Now, armed with the word of the Lord, Jehoshaphat organized the armies in an unusual way. He sent the worshipers out ahead of the warriors. They released the sound of praise and partnered with the word of the Lord for victory declaring, "Praise the LORD, for His mercy endures forever" (verse 21). In the midst of the atmosphere created by this sound, the enemy armies turned on one another and destroyed each other, leaving so much wealth it took Judah three days to gather it up! The sound created breakthrough.

What do these scenarios all have in common? In each instance the people all heard the prophetic strategy through the voice of the Lord, they all made a sound, a proclamation, decree or praise and heaven responded by fighting for them. The Breaker arose and brought victory when the people created a sound.

## Break Through and Go Beyond

Each of these stories tells of a military encounter, which is the picture God gives of the concept of breakthrough. The word *breakthrough* is actually a military term, which the dictionary defines as "a military movement or advance all the way through and beyond an enemy's front-line defense."[1] We must go through and beyond. I think the Church has been pretty good at breaking through, but not always as good at going beyond. We press in through prayer to receive a miracle, a healing or a provision. Once we have broken through and received our answer, however, true breakthrough dictates that we become the breaker for others. We have pressed in and warred for our healing, now we must become healers. We have contended for financial breakthrough, now we must extend our Kingdom influence so others can break out of poverty and lack as well. Our miracle becomes the catalyst for others to experience God's supernatural power. We must go through so that we can go beyond.

A great example of this occurred during World War II when the Allied Forces landed on the beaches of Normandy on D-Day. The enemy's line was fortified, yet through great sacrifice and strength the soldiers stormed the beaches and broke through that frontline of defense. Once the soldiers achieved victory, however, they did not stop and put their weapons down and have a party. Why? Because their goal was never just to break through, but rather to go beyond. There were cities and nations that cried out to be set free. There were oppressors who needed to be vanquished. Because of the breakthrough

104

they now had a beachhead to be the freedom force that would change the world.

So it is in the Church. We may be facing down an opposing force that seems fortified and fierce; however, God has anointed us for breakthrough. We are to contend with our hearts, our words and our spirits to win personal victories, and then we use those miracles as platforms from which we go beyond, outside the walls of our churches to liberate people wherever we go. We are heaven's freedom force called to go through and beyond every frontline defense of the enemy.

## Removing the Barriers to Progress

We see that *breakthrough* can be a military term. The dictionary definition goes on to say that a breakthrough is also the "act or instance of removing or surpassing an obstruction or restriction; the overcoming of a stalemate; any significant or sudden advance, development, achievement, or increase, as in scientific knowledge or diplomacy, that removes a barrier to progress."[2]

The day I heard the Lord say, *Tell them the Breaker is here,* I knew God was saying that He was going to fight for us and help us overcome some seemingly insurmountable odds. There had been an economic downturn and some in our congregation were facing either foreclosure or bankruptcy. Our ministry had big plans and a vision for the future; however, it seemed as though we were stuck with no possible way forward. Yet God had said He was there as our Breaker. He further said to me, *Tell the people not to accept what seems to be inevitable. Release your faith, and I will do the impossible.* Great faith was stirred in our service that day as people came out of agreement with disaster and instead agreed with the decree of the Lord. Our Breaker was there, and we knew He would fight for us.

Over the next several months we saw things turn around in miraculous ways. Some individuals received financial miracles; some received healing in their bodies, others in their marriages. Businesses that looked doomed to close were suddenly infused with new vision that enabled them to move out of restriction and into growth and increase. Disrupted destinies were once again aligned and set on course for a successful future. It truly became a breakout season for many.

## Your Breaker Is Here

Now is the time! God stands ready as your Breaker to break off all limitations. Receive His anointing for breakthrough. God is creating a momentum of breakthrough for your family, your health, your vision, your destiny, your finances and the purpose of His people, the Church. The Breaker is here, and He has gone up before us.

─────────── YOUR DECLARATION ───────────

*My Breaker is here for me now. Because Jesus goes before me, all confinement and all restrictions are coming off. Every limitation is being broken, and I am free to move forward, to advance, to break out and to break through. I am free to become a success. I am free to prosper. God is giving me divine strategies to remove every barrier that stands in the way of my progress. I am not stuck; I am going through and beyond every hindrance so I can set others free. I decree this in the name of Jesus, my Breaker. My Breaker is here. My victory is here. My breakthrough is here. So I will shout to the Lord and release my sound of breakthrough. (Now shout to the Lord!)*

## YOUR ACTIVATION

What limitation do you want to see Jesus, your Breaker, break off of your life? Once you identify this area, create a sound of breakthrough by either decreeing, praising or shouting. Remember, your breakthrough has a sound.

# Divine Reversals

"The LORD your God turned the curse into a blessing for you, because the LORD your God loves you."

Deuteronomy 23:5

During one of our conferences I prophesied that God was bringing "divine reversals" into the lives of His people. Among other things the Lord said that He was causing "divine reversals" in physical conditions of deterioration and turning them around. This was God's decree that would release healing.

One of our young ministers, Rebecca Francis, later gave public testimony that she had experienced a divine reversal in her eye that night. Though she was only in her late twenties, she had a pressure imbalance that was progressively causing her to lose her vision. Each time she visited the doctor the area of blindness was found to have increased. The prognosis was that this would continue until she lost all sight in her eye.

The day after I prophesied "divine reversals" in areas of degeneration, she returned to her doctor, who was astounded. The pressure in her eye was normal, and all lost vision was restored.

The prophetic word that I decreed was not spontaneous but rather came from something God had spoken to me a few weeks earlier, which resulted in a spectacular miracle for one of my grandchildren. You might recall this story from a previous book. As it continues to inspire and inform my decrees, I would like to share it with you again.

I was in my office praying and seeking the Lord early one morning when I heard Him say to tell the people of God that He has begun releasing "divine reversals," that He is beginning to turn things around for His people—health, finances, prodigals, families, ministries, businesses and even nations. It will be a time for turnaround miracles. Things that seemed impossible before are now being made possible because we are entering a time of divine intervention and grace. God has heard the cry of His people!

A few hours later Tom and I got a call from one of our children saying something was wrong with their son. He had previously been diagnosed with a severe compression on his brain and would need surgery. Because of some other physical challenges, however, they could not operate for at least another six months. The parents were told that one of the dangers was he could lose the use of an arm or leg, and, if that occurred, the damage would be irreversible. The day God spoke to me about "divine reversals," my grandson had lost the use of his left leg.

We brought the family to our house and declared divine reversal over our boy. The first day, nothing happened. The second day, his condition got worse. But on the third day he jumped out of bed and began running around the house, completely restored!

So I began diligently to study the biblical concept of "divine reversals." Deuteronomy 23:5 says that the Lord will turn curse to blessing for us because He loves us. Psalm 30:11 speaks of God turning our mourning to dancing. First Samuel 10:6 tells of the time when Samuel told Saul that he was about to meet a company of prophets along the road: "The Spirit of the LORD will come upon you, and you will prophesy with them and be turned into another man."

All these verses use the Hebraic word for *reversal, haphak*, which means "to turn, to turn around, to overthrow, to change, to reverse, to transform oneself" (*Strong's* 2015). It can be used for personal inner transformation, as with Saul, as a military term indicating overthrowing an enemy kingdom or to indicate the presence of God's hand to turn evil intention into divine purpose. In the book of Esther we see it used in the sense of reversing a decree of death and destruction and releasing a new decree of authority, life and peace.

When God spoke to me initially about "divine reversals" I was studying the book of Esther. This story helps us understand the authority we have been given to shift entire cultures through the power of the decree. As we endeavor to write and speak what God decrees, here are some directives that I believe will increase our effectiveness to bring "divine reversals."

## 1. Take Up the Call to Intercede

Esther is a prophetic picture of the Church, the followers of Christ, who are interceding for nations and generations today. The book of Esther is the story of a young Jewish woman living in captivity in Persia, who was made queen. Shortly after this event it was discovered that a wicked man named Haman (not to be confused with Hamon, as that is my name!) had written a decree against the Jewish people to wipe them off the face of the earth and to take all their property. Esther's relative and guardian, Mordecai, asked Esther to go before the king to intercede for a reversal of this death decree.

The word *intercession* describes a prayer or petition in favor of someone else. The person who intercedes acts as a go-between to help solve a problem. It also describes someone who intervenes to bring help.[1] The word *intervene* paints the picture of true intercession. It means "to come between opposing sides, to jump into the middle of something to interfere, to get involved so as to alter or hinder an action through force or threat of force."[2] In other words, an intercessor gets in the way and interrupts the devil's plan. This is exactly what Esther did and what we are called to do.

Today there is great hostility against believers and the cause of Christ in the earth, and it seems to be growing worse. The devil would love to see wickedness and injustice prevail and the voice of righteousness and truth silenced. We are living in the day where good is called evil and evil good (see Isaiah 5:20). God is looking for intercessors who will jump into the middle of things in prayer, get in the way of the devil's plans and cause things to turn around.

The king in the story of Esther was named Ahasuerus, which means "I will keep you poor and silent" (*Strong's* 325). This is the strategy of the enemy against the Church today. In today's media and culture, prayer and faith are mocked in an attempt to intimidate and silence the voice of God's people and to rob us of having any influence on our culture. But God has a plan! The pendulum is swinging, and the enemy is overplaying his hand. God's Church is rising in power to intercede and get in the way of the enemy's plan. The curse is getting ready to be turned to a blessing for us.

We must always remember that Jesus became a curse for us so we do not have to live under a curse (see Galatians 3:13). He was the master of divine reversal. Everything He did demonstrated God's power to turn death to life, sickness to health, lack to blessing, etc. We have been given the power to act as intercessors, frontline warriors, those called to get in the way of the enemy's devices. We need to decree freedom and blessing and extend that freedom to others by reversing the curses of darkness as we pray and decree heaven's purposes into the earth.

## 2. Spend Your Favor

One time while I was prophesying to someone I heard the Lord say, *I have given you favor; now I am going to teach you to spend My favor.* What a powerful concept!

When Esther approached the throne, the king stretched out his scepter of favor to her (see Esther 5:1–3). We can picture this as the Church approaching the throne of the Lord and receiving favor. In addition, when we have favor with God, we can ask Him to give us favor with others.

It is often said that faith is the currency of heaven, meaning that as we spend our faith before God He hears our prayers and pours out the resources of heaven over our lives. I believe, however, that favor is currency to be used with people here on earth. As we spend our favor we are given answers to those things we seek; we see doors opened and opportunities afforded. These are spiritual powers that bring natural breakthroughs.

One of the ways I like to describe what it means to have favor is that people will be drawn to you supernaturally, want to be around you and want to know what you think. They will want to promote you and show you goodwill. They will want to give you opportunity and position. I believe this is a picture of the people of God approaching the thrones of influence in this world system and receiving amazing opportunities to bring change. We need to learn to receive favor from God and then spend it in order to advance God's Kingdom and to open doors of influence that would otherwise remain closed.

> So it was, when the king saw Queen Esther standing in the court, that she found favor in his sight, and the king held out to Esther the golden scepter that was in his hand. Then Esther went near and touched the top of the scepter. And the king said to her, "What do you wish, Queen Esther? What is your request? It shall be given to you—up to half the kingdom!"
>
> Esther 5:2–3

So Esther asked the king to come to a banquet with Haman. She was getting positioned for the Big Ask. The king came to her banquet, where Esther served him. We need to learn to serve those in position in the world systems and show them the heart of Christ. Serving produces favor. As a result of her serving him the king asked again,

> "What is your petition? It shall be granted you. What is your request, up to half the kingdom? It shall be done!"
>
> Then Esther answered and said, "My petition and request is this: If I have found favor in the sight of the king, and if it pleases the king to grant my petition and fulfill my request then. . . ."
>
> Esther 5:6–8

Esther was saying, "If I really have favor with you, King, then here is how I want to spend it!"

113

We need to understand that there is a difference between *having* favor and *spending* favor. You can have money and not spend it. You can also have favor and not spend it . . . or not spend it wisely. It is time for the people of God to recognize that we have been given amazing favor through our relationship with Christ.

Tom and I received a call one day from Sharon Parkes, an elder in our church who was on her way to the hospital for emergency surgery on her eye for a detached retina. She was carrying the films from her initial doctor's diagnosis and was asking for prayer.

We began to decree divine reversal over her eye, in the name of Jesus, asking boldly for a miracle. When Sharon got to the hospital the medical personnel reviewed the films and said she definitely had a detached retina. They took their own set of films as part of the preparation for emergency surgery. But then a doctor came in and spent a great deal of time examining her eye, looking first at one set of films then the other.

Finally he said, "I don't know what has happened, but you do not have a detached retina. The first set of films clearly shows you do, but the second set and now my examination find no evidence of it. This is one for the record books."

It certainly was! It was evidence of divine reversals that come in Jesus' name as we approach His throne of favor boldly.

As I began preaching about divine reversals, many people in our church began to see prodigals turning around and coming home, financial disasters and bankruptcies averted, legal situations settled, barrenness broken off so babies were born, businesses that were failing turned around and prospering, sicknesses healed, health restored and even the dead brought back to life. All these things happened because people heard the word of the Lord, faith arose in their hearts and they began to say what God said—and divine reversals were the result.

In the New Testament the words *grace* and *favor* come from the same Greek word *charis.* So when Scripture says to come boldly before God's throne of grace, it is for far more than just forgiveness of our sins; it is also a throne of favor: "Let us therefore come boldly to the throne of grace, that we may obtain mercy and find grace to help in time of need" (Hebrews 4:16).

It is a throne of *favor* (*charis* . . . grace, favor, graciousness, joy, pleasure, delight, sweetness, goodwill, benefit, loving-kindness, gifts, rewards, strength and increase), which we can come before *boldly* (*parrhesia* . . . with free and fearless confidence, with freedom and boldness of speech, open, honest, blunt, with cheerful courage), to lay hold of *mercy* (*eleos* . . . kindness or goodwill toward the miserable and the afflicted, joined with a desire to help them) and to find *help* (*boétheia* . . . a military term, a call to battle to help someone who is struggling) in a time of need. We come boldly before God's throne of grace/favor and ask boldly for what is needed—for ourselves or for others. It is again, a picture of intercession.[3]

If ever the people of God needed favor to impact our world, that time is now. We need God's help in our nations. We need God's help in our families. We need God's help to do the work of the Kingdom and to see a mighty harvest of souls. We also need favor with our fellow man if we are to have open doors of opportunity and walk in the influence that shifts cultures.

### 3. Write a New Decree

In this process of divine reversal in the story of Esther, God began to set Haman up to have his wickedness exposed so that the only option would be for the king to destroy him. Watch for exposure to happen more and more as God uncovers corruption, wickedness and other plans devised in darkness.

But even though Haman was executed, his decree of destruction remained. This process was not just about destroying an opponent but also about cutting off the entire scheme he had set into motion; in other words, Haman's decree of darkness still had legal ground to perpetuate the curse.

When Esther approached the king again in order to have the decree of Haman revoked, the king responded with these words:

> "You yourselves write a decree concerning the Jews, as you please, in the king's name, and seal it with the king's signet ring; for whatever is written in the king's name and sealed with the king's signet ring no one can revoke."
>
> Esther 8:8

We need to write new decrees. The enemy has declared things over our personal lives, over the Church today and over our nations. He is filling the airwaves in the spirit realm and in the natural realm with decrees of fear, unrighteousness, death, defeat, destruction and intimidation.

Initially, when Esther first learned of Haman's evil plan, Mordecai shook her out of her fear by saying,

> "If you remain completely silent at this time, relief and deliverance will arise for the Jews from another place, but you and your father's house will perish. Yet who knows whether you have come to the kingdom for such a time as this?"
>
> Esther 4:14

Today we are in an Esther moment. The Church cannot be silent. Nations are hanging in the balance. We must make decrees in prayer. Write one down. Let it be your confession. We must uproot unrighteous decrees and write new decrees that speak to God's purposes and plans.

We must decree God's Word in truth, knowing that the penetrating power of truth can set others free. We must change our language to reflect what God is declaring. We must allow prophetic words to be in our mouths as decrees. Say what God says! We may need to write letters, make phone calls or even go to court to get certain reversals. And if we find ourselves in the public spotlight, standing before the kings and rulers of this world, we must have the wisdom of Esther and Mordecai to speak words that will turn curses to blessings. We must spend our favor to turn hearts.

In this time of great darkness, the people of God need to flood the atmosphere with decrees that drive out death and darkness—that bring life and light. We must begin to control the narrative in the spirit, lest the enemy's plans control the narrative in the natural.

## 4. Fight Back

What decree did Esther and Mordecai write? They wrote a decree authorizing God's people to fight back. They were allowed to "destroy, kill, and annihilate all the forces of any people or province that would assault them" (see Esther 8:11).

I know this does not seem to go along with Jesus' admonition to turn the other cheek, but this is not about fighting and destroying people; it is about overthrowing rulers of darkness. It is about unjust, antichrist systems (antichrist means "against Christ") that must turn around. We can have no mercy on the spirits of darkness (see Deuteronomy 7:1–2). We are not helpless or hopeless. We can always fight back by employing our spiritual weapons to see triumph. We are entering times of great victory, but we must partner with the Lord to see the reversals. "Now thanks be to God who always leads us in triumph in Christ, and through us diffuses the fragrance of His knowledge in every place" (2 Corinthians 2:14).

## 5. Receive Divine Reversals

We see the reversal for the Jews manifested fully in the ninth chapter of Esther. It begins by saying: "On the very day when the enemies of the Jews hoped to [overpower] gain the mastery over them, the reverse occurred; [and instead] the Jews [overpowered] gained mastery over those who hated them" (Esther 9:1 ESV).

An entire nation was saved that day. At the moment of crisis, God turned everything around for His people. We are living in a similar time of divine reversal; God wants to turn things around for us. God wants to turn nations around in this tipping-point moment. It looked as though the Jews were headed for disaster, but God turned it around for them. He will do the same for us.

As a matter of fact, I heard the Lord say that this will be a "boomerang season." In the Message translation Esther 9:25 reads: "When Queen Esther intervened with the king, he gave written orders that the evil scheme that Haman had worked out should boomerang back on his own head." Haman built gallows to hang Mordecai, but he ended up being hanged on them himself (see Esther 7:9–10). And not only was Haman destroyed, but his ten sons were also killed so they could not retaliate. God is going to cause every curse and every assignment thrown out from hell to turn right back upon the head of our spiritual enemy.

God is going to turn curses into blessings for us because He loves us.

Here in the United States of America, God has determined to bring some significant "divine reversals," turning us back to a place of righteousness and justice. There is a rising feeling of "Enough is enough!" God is awakening His people from complacency and even raising up non-believing advocates for truth and righteousness in the media and marketplace who will be bold enough to take a stand and shift the status quo.

## 6. Release Sounds of Joy

Esther 9 describes the Jews' celebration upon the defeat of their enemies: the initiation of the Feast of Purim. This annual event is also called the "holiday of reversals" for mourning was turned to great joy. The decree of death and destruction was turned instead to blessing and promotion. Mordecai was placed second in rank to the king himself and was held in high esteem by his fellow Jews. He and Esther, in their positions of authority, had heightened potential to influence the future.

Jesus came and personally defeated the decree of death and destruction over our lives—the ultimate turnaround—so that we can live in perpetual divine reversal. The Gospel is truly a divine reversal story. When the enemy nailed Jesus to the cross, he thought he had won, but the greatest divine reversal in all of history was already in progress. Jesus was slain from the foundation of the world. God had a plan. After three days, Jesus turned death to life and tragedy to victory. He continues to do the same today.

Jewish families celebrate the Feast of Purim by giving gifts to one another, by helping the poor and by recounting the story of Esther. It is interesting to note that the observance of Purim was outlawed in Nazi Germany during the reign of Hitler. The powerful story of God's deliverance of His people threatened the Nazi agenda.[4]

Today, when Jewish people celebrate Purim and read aloud the book of Esther, they use noisemakers and shouting to drown out the sound of Haman's name. Just so, God wants the sound of celebration and joy in the mouths of His people to drown out the sound of the enemy.

We must be very intentional about this type of celebration: There is power in the sound of joy.

God is turning mourning to dancing and sorrow to joy. He is giving us beauty for ashes, the oil of joy for mourning and the garment of praise for the spirit of heaviness. Will you partner with Him for "divine reversals"? Hear the decree of the Lord: Take up the call to intercede—to intervene and to interrupt the enemy's plans. Spend your favor both with God and with your fellow human beings. Write a new decree over your life, your family and your city. Fight back, using your spiritual weapons in this spiritual battle. Receive divine reversals—reversals in health, in finances and in your destiny. Release the sounds of joy, celebration and expectation. It is time!

## YOUR DECLARATION

*This is my time of divine reversal. Whatever the enemy has meant against me for evil is being turned for my good. Whatever schemes the enemy has formed in secret will be uncovered and boomerang back on his own head. I will spend my favor and expect to see new open doors of opportunity so I can advance the Kingdom of God and my destiny. I will write new decrees and join them with my prayers of intercession to see breakthrough happen. God will turn my mourning to dancing, my sorrow to joy, my sickness to health, my lack to abundance and my doubt to faith. God is turning things around for me!*

## YOUR ASSIGNMENT

Think of an area of your life in which you need to see a divine reversal. Write a decree using Scriptures about what your turnaround will look like. Speak this decree out loud as part of your daily devotions until you see things change.

# Agreeing with the Voice of God

The voice of the Lord is powerful.

Psalm 29:4

People often ask me how to know what they should be declaring. It is very easy: Declare the word of the Lord. Declare the Scriptures. Declare what He speaks to you through dreams, visions and angelic visitations, through reading the Word, through hearing someone preach the Word, through His still, small voice. As we hear the word of the Lord and begin to declare it, we are not only agreeing with the word but also waging spiritual warfare against any spiritual force trying to keep the word from coming to pass.

Some people tend to receive audible words from the Lord; others hear God speaking through visions or pictures; still others receive revelation by sensing or feeling something. The word of the Lord can come through many of the gifts of the Holy Spirit who dwells within. Here are a few ways God has spoken to me, some examples of how I discerned the meaning of what He said, and then the corresponding declarations I wrote to agree with the voice of God.

## The Voice of the Lord through Visions

As I was praying one day I had a vision of Jesus handing out white stones to believers who were pressing in to overcome and bring God's Kingdom into the earth. He looked each believer in the eye, placed the white stone in his or her hand, closed his or her hand around it and then nodded, as if to say, "I've got this."

When I receive a vision like this, I go immediately to the Bible to search for something similar that might help me gain understanding. I found an important picture in the book of Revelation, as the Lord directs John to write this revelation "to the angel of the church in Pergamos":

> "He who has an ear, let him hear what the Spirit says to the churches. To him who overcomes I will give some of the hidden manna to eat. And I will give him a white stone, and on the stone a new name written which no one knows except him who receives it."
>
> Revelation 2:17

This is a mysterious passage of Scripture written to a congregation in the city of Pergamum, where the seat of Satan was located. It was a city of deep idolatry and demonic thrones of iniquity; but more concerning was the compromise of righteousness being allowed in the fellowship. Some held the "doctrine of Balaam," which caused people to have no concern about eating food sacrificed to idols in situations where they would be further seduced to partake of idolatrous rites and embrace the practice of sexual immorality without consequence (i.e., compromising with the world). This church also harbored those of the Nicolaitan cult, which taught that because Christians were no longer under the law but under grace, they could live in any sinful manner they chose.

God was very clear that He hated these doctrines, and that if they did not repent He would come and "fight against them with the sword of [His] mouth" (Revelation 2:16).

The power of our words will cause God to speak words of blessing and favor, and to fight for us, but He will also confront us with sin and even fight against us with a sword from His own mouth if we fail to align with the truth of His righteousness. This is a time of righteousness, purifying and alignment for the overcoming Church. Jesus says that to those who overcome He will give the hidden manna (symbolizing a release of provision, revelation and life) and give them a white stone with a new name written on it.

Years ago the Lord said to me, *The only way you become an overcomer is that you actually have something that you have to overcome.* Whatever you are currently facing, you are in the time of overcoming . . . pressing in with faith—not fear—praying, decreeing, prophesying and worshiping. You will overcome by the words of your mouth. The victory is in your mouth. The miracle you need is in your mouth.

In the first century, people understood that a white stone was a symbol of favor and overcoming against the odds. In a trial the jury members would cast their votes by dropping into a box either a white stone for acquittal or a black stone for punishment. When elections were held in a city, people would cast their votes by dropping in a white stone for yes, a black stone for no. In athletic games, the winner of a contest was given a white stone identifying the bearer as a champion or overcomer. This white stone acted as a ticket or a pass giving that athlete access to places of honor at events and position in society. From that time forward, that citizen was no longer an ordinary citizen, but rather a super-citizen, with celebrity status.[1]

After I had the vision, a year followed in which we faced some unprecedented crises in the world. I knew that God gives us encouragement or affirmation for having overcome hardships in the past; rather, though, this was a prophecy that we would overcome in times of great trial in the present and future. Jesus was prophesying to the church at Pergamum then, and to us today, saying, "I have acquitted you of your sin; I have cast My vote for your success, and no matter what you face, you can overcome!" First John 5:4–5 declares, "Whatever is born of God overcomes the world. And this is the victory that has overcome the world—our faith. Who is he who overcomes the world, but he who believes that Jesus is the Son of God?"

Jesus told His disciples, who He knew would face incredible trials and persecution, this: "Everything I've taught you is so that the peace which is in me will be in you and will give you great confidence as you rest in me. For in this unbelieving world you will experience trouble and sorrows, but you must be courageous, for I have conquered the world!" (John 16:33 TPT).

In order to be an overcomer we must run the race and win. In my vision God was giving us the white stone of the overcomer before we ever faced a crisis. God was giving us His vote of confidence, saying, "You can do this! You can prevail! You can overcome!" The Greek word for *overcome* is the word *nikaó*, which means "to subdue, conquer, overcome, prevail, get the victory" (*Strong's* 3528). It is from the root word *niké*—the name of the brand of athletic wear with the famous slogan "Just do it!"

Today God is looking for an overcoming Church: one who refuses to compromise with pressure to conform to the world and its philosophies and doctrines; one who will stand up against the throne of Satan and all his darkness and witchcraft, and will stand for truth, holiness and unwavering faith in the face of persecution. God is looking for those who will not give place to fear but will continue to put their trust in Him. God will fight for those who stand for Him. To them He will give a white stone of favor, which will open new doors for Kingdom access even in the kingdoms of men.

Ask for your new name. Allow God to speak fresh understanding of destiny, calling and identity over your life to shift you into your new season.

─────────── **YOUR DECLARATION** ───────────

*I am an overcomer—for the One who has overcome all dwells in me. Any time I experience trials or tribulations I will be happy because Jesus has already overcome the world. I will overcome every false doctrine, power of darkness, sin, occult force, oppression, depression or fear that stands in my way. (Feel free to insert your own words of what you expect to overcome.) No weapon formed against me shall prosper in any way. I am a champion. I am not a victim but a victor through Christ. I receive my white stone of favor and victory from the Lord. Now doors will open to me, giving me access to places in culture so I can carry influence for God's Kingdom. In Jesus' name!*

## The Voice of the Lord through Dreams

I had a dream in which a demonic assignment was sent against a godly leader and reformer. The enemy's name was Rabshakeh, and he was coming to spread poison on the back of the leader, then take a rod and beat his back, driving the poison in until this reformer broke. (The back represents the place of a person's strength. The back was where Jesus was beaten so that we can receive our healing.) The enemy wanted to beat down this leader, afflict him with poison, rob from him and destroy him. But before Rabshakeh could complete his mission of destruction, we alerted the authorities, who captured him. They then led us out and put the enemy's rod into our hands to beat the back of our enemy!

When I awoke from this dream I laughed. I was thinking that *Rabshakeh* was probably the name of a reggae band and that I had eaten too much pizza the night before. To my amazement, however, I found the story of Rabshakeh in 2 Kings 18, Isaiah 36 and 2 Chronicles 32. This story tells of the besiegement of Jerusalem during the rulership of Hezekiah, a righteous king who was bringing reformation to the tribe of Judah and turning them back to righteousness and true worship. Sennacherib, the king of Assyria, surrounded the city and sent his emissary, his mouthpiece, Rabshakeh, out to deliver terms of surrender.

*Rabshakeh* means "chief prince"; it signifies a demonic assignment against reformers, leaders, believers and even nations today. He represents the voice of the devil, trying to defeat believers by implanting words of doubt in their minds. In the hearing of the people of Israel, he filled the atmosphere with demoralizing words of accusation, telling them they were foolish to trust their God to save them or their king to deliver them. He tried to convince them their situation was impossible, that God had forsaken them and that they had no option other than to give up. He even prophesied that it was God who had sent Assyria to destroy Judah.

Sounds just like the devil, right? Understand that he was seeking to spread the poison of lies so that they would be beaten down and submit to giving up and being overthrown. Today I believe Rabshakeh rides on the airwaves of the media, saturating the atmosphere over cities and nations, spewing his false narrative in order to gain dominance, causing people to be confused, to compromise and to give up their stand for righteousness.

Never let the enemy get into your head! There is such a thing as demonic mind control that tries to talk believers out of their destinies. The devil will try to convince you that all your works of righteousness and reformation have been for nothing, and that in the end God will not hear your prayers and will abandon you. The devil will try to wear you down and wear you out with these accusations, intimidations and frustrations so that all your strength is exhausted. Rather than being a nation changer you seek just to survive. He tries to get into the heads of God's reformers, tries to define the narrative, beating them down by relentlessly filling the atmosphere with lies and accusations. Beware of what you hear and what you believe, for Rabshakeh is active as the devil's mouthpiece to beat down God's anointed.

After my initial reaction to the dream of laughing, I realized that it was all too real as I entered my own battle with this spirit. I experienced strange sicknesses, weariness and relentless accusatory thoughts bombarding my mind. It was one of the most powerful demonic attacks I have ever experienced.

My husband and leaders prayed for me, and I took captive every thought and made it obedient to Christ (see 2 Corinthians 10:5)—and I experienced victory. Over the next several months I met and ministered to more ministers who were battling with the same things. Some were so depressed they were suicidal.

This dream brought discernment to uncover tactics and strategies of the enemy to bring down anointed leaders and believers and bring them into defeat.

### From Besiegement to Breakthrough

Rather than let Rabshakeh and his poisonous words of accusation and mind control rob God's people of their land, Hezekiah set himself to seek the Lord and to pray. When Sennacherib had first laid siege to Jerusalem, Hezekiah had encouraged his people by speaking these faith-filled words in the midst of desperate times:

> Be strong and courageous, be not afraid nor dismayed for the king of Assyria, nor for all the multitude that is with him: for there be more with us than with him: With him is an arm of flesh; but with us is the LORD our God to help us, and to fight our battles. And the people rested themselves upon the words of Hezekiah king of Judah.
>
> 2 Chronicles 32:7–8 KJV

The Church would do well to allow these words to encourage us during our challenging times.

Hezekiah went to the Temple, laid the accusations of the enemy before God and cried out to Him (see 2 Kings 19:14–19). I felt the Lord challenge me that often we come to the altar, but it is actually an altar made out of our questions and offenses because God has allowed hard things to happen—an altar of "whys." We think we are coming to pray, but we are really coming to complain and accuse God. I really believe that God said these are idolatrous altars of our own making and must be torn down. We must stop asking why and instead repent and put our trust in the Lord. God is after our hearts in this season and stands ready to answer our cries; however, we must humble ourselves as Hezekiah did—and then he saw God's mighty deliverance.

As Hezekiah prayed, he also sent for Isaiah the prophet to get a word from God. This is the synergy that comes when government, prayer and the prophetic anointing create a dynamic for breakthrough. Isaiah came and told Hezekiah that the Lord had heard his prayers. He would defend the city! He then released a prophetic word of breakthrough— that, frankly, sounded impossible—with the encouragement that God would fight for His people. That night God sent an angel down who wiped out 185,000 Assyrians. Sennacherib returned to his country only to be killed by two of his own sons.

God fought for Judah! Dedicated prayer and powerful prophecy shifted the battle and brought heavenly intervention. Victory was manifested as God mobilized the angel armies to overthrow the enemy.

If we will position ourselves as Hezekiah did and set ourselves to seek the Lord, to hear the prophetic word of the Lord over our lives and to put our trust in Him to fight for us, we will see every voice of the accuser struck down, every mind-binding spirit broken, every besiegement destroyed and everything stolen returned in abundance. Hezekiah's name means "Jehovah is my strength." In this time of contending for the Kingdom of God to be advanced in the earth, God will restore our strength physically, emotionally and spiritually so we can run the race we are called to.

### The Voice of the Lord Shatters the Enemy

If you recall at the end of my dream the rod of punishment that the enemy sought to use against the leader was instead used on his own back. The Lord turns the evil that the enemy sends against us back on his own head. Isaiah also prophesied about this, which is part of God's battle strategy for us today to break out of the survival of besiegement into revival for a new day:

> The voice of the LORD will shatter Assyria [your enemy]; with his scepter he will strike them down. Every stroke the LORD lays [on the back of the enemy] with his punishing rod will be to the music of tambourines and harps, as he fights them in battle with the blows of his arm.
>
> Isaiah 30:31–32 NIV1984

The voice of the Lord and our praise is a weapon.

So rise up, reformers! Lift up your heads, leaders! Seek the Lord and hear His voice. Whatever it is that you are battling, shake off every shroud of discouragement and fear, resist every Rabshakeh assignment to get into your head through accusations and lies and watch as the voice of the Lord shatters your enemy. Wage warfare with your prophecies; every tongue (Rabshakeh) that has risen up against you shall be condemned. Today is the day God is arising to send down angel armies to fight for you.

--------- YOUR DECLARATION ---------

*My life is hidden with Christ in God (see Colossians 3:3); therefore, no strategy of hell can defeat me. I declare that I will discern any tactic of the enemy formed against me so I can rise up in the strength of Christ to defeat it. Rabshakeh has no control over my life. I break every assignment against my physical body and will live and walk in health. I break off every mind-binding, mind-controlling spirit trying to drag me down, and I rise up in the victory found in Christ Jesus. I cast out every lie of the accuser and will fill the atmosphere over my life with praise, worship, prayers and decrees. When I face impossible odds, God will fight for me. He will even send angels down to help me. I will let God's word be in my mouth and will prophesy against my enemy—and the voice of the Lord will shatter my enemy. I declare this in Jesus' name.*

### The Inspired Voice of God

As I mentioned, God speaks in a variety of ways: through His written Word, through dreams, visions, angels and even through an audible voice. God also speaks through others, who might say something that lights up your heart with revelation. This could be a testimony of something the Lord has done for someone, a story or illustration, or perhaps a message someone is preaching. When I am preaching I often encourage people to touch their ears and ask the voice of the Lord to be louder in their ears than anything I am saying. Here is an example of God speaking to me through an anointed word I heard preached through a fellow prophet.

Rachel Hickson is a prophet from the U.K. whom I have had the pleasure to hear on a few occasions. She carries an amazing mantle of leadership, strategy and prophetic insight. In one message that particularly inspired me she mentioned the concept of the "super bloom." She said that Flanders Field in Belgium is famous for all the poppies that sprang up after the agitating of the soil with boots and bloodshed during the trench warfare of World War I. She taught that it takes harsh conditions, drought, fire, flood, etc. to agitate the seed and wake it up for a super bloom.

Super blooms occur in desert regions—dry, barren terrains. The seeds blow in on the wind and land on ground so parched that the seeds actually settle down into the cracks and crevices, going deep into the earth and lying dormant for sometimes as long as ten to fifteen years. Then some sort of agitation, crisis or calamity shakes or stirs the ground and awakens the seeds and . . . *bam!* Super bloom!

Right before I heard this I had a dream in which God spoke to me declaring a season of "crazy increase," a season of super-abundance. I felt that this message was confirmation of the times and season the Body of Christ was coming into, and I heard the Lord say, *Watch for the super blooms. Expect the super blooms.*

That year I began to keep an eye on the California desert—and it had a super bloom. I discovered super blooms had occurred in three of the last four years. These are normally experienced only once every ten to fifteen years; super blooms were happening on an accelerated rate.

In February 2020 the Dead Sea area of Israel experienced its first super bloom in history. One headline in the Israeli media read, "Dead Sea Blooms Floral Wonderland for First Time"[2] and "Rains Bring Stunning Displays to Parched Dead Sea Area."[3] The Dead Sea is full of salt and the land is some of the harshest on earth, yet the area burst into beautiful fields of flowers. This is what God can do in our lives. He can bring rain on our dry ground and cause our desert places to bloom like the rose.

Hear these promises from the Lord:

The wilderness and dry land will be joyously glad! The desert will blossom like a rose and rejoice! Every dry and barren place will burst forth with abundant blossoms, dancing and spinning with delight! Lebanon's lush splendor covers it, the magnificent beauty of Carmel and Sharon. My people will see the awesome glory of Yahweh, the beautiful grandeur of our God.

Strengthen those who are discouraged. Energize those who feel defeated. Say to the anxious and fearful, "Be strong and never afraid. Look, here comes your God! He is breaking through to give you victory! He comes to avenge your enemies. With divine retribution he comes to save you!"

Then blind eyes will open and deaf ears will hear. Then the lame will leap like playful deer and the tongue-tied will sing songs of triumph. Gushing water will spring up in the wilderness and streams will flow through the desert. The burning sand will become a refreshing oasis, the parched ground bubbling springs. . . .

There will be a highway of holiness called the Sacred Way. The impure will not be permitted on this road, but it will be accessible to God's people. And not even fools will lose their way. The lion will not be found there; no wild beast will travel on it— they will not be found there. But the redeemed will find a pathway on it. Yahweh's ransomed ones will return with glee to Zion. They will enter with a song of rejoicing and be crowned with everlasting joy. Ecstatic joy will overwhelm them.

Isaiah 35 TPT

During the COVID-19 global shutdown in 2020, I was very concerned for some of the business owners in our church. Since we live in a beach area, many of our businesses make the majority of their money for the year between March and August, the tourist season. But all tourists were banned from our area, and all these businesses were closed. It was a desperate situation.

But as soon as the beaches opened, I began hearing reports from these business owners. "We are making twice the money we made last year," some said. "Business is booming," said others. "God has given us some new strategies so we can work smarter not harder, and it is paying off with amazing increase."

One restaurant owner said, "It's crazy! We are allowed to operate only at fifty-percent capacity, but I am making more money this year than last year. All my bills are paid, and I have even been able to pay off some debt." I heard from other business people in our church who said they were landing new contracts at the most unusual times. Each one claimed that God had brought a super bloom into their businesses, lives and families. During this time of the pandemic shutdown, we continued to declare super bloom, and eighteen families in our church bought new homes. He is a God of miracles.

You may be in one of the driest, most difficult times of your life, but God is getting ready to send the rain of His presence in abundance to wake up the seeds of destiny, prosperity and purpose within you.

*Your place of trial is becoming your place of triumph.*
*Your place of barrenness is becoming your place of blessing.*
*Your wilderness is becoming your place of victory.*
*Your opposition is becoming your place of opportunity.*
*Every place of delay and dormancy is becoming a place of a super-abundant super bloom.*

It is time for "crazy increase"!

### YOUR DECLARATION

*This is my super-bloom season. Things may look dry and difficult, but God is causing my life to bloom like the rose. He is strengthening me when I feel discouraged and energizing me when I feel defeated. I will be strong and courageous, for my God is breaking through to give me victory. My place of trial is my place of triumph. Every place that looks like barrenness is bursting forth into blessing. My opposition has become my opportunity. I declare that all the seeds I have sown in prayer, in decreeing and in giving, which have been lying dormant, are waking up to bless me and accomplish their purpose. It is my time of super-abundance. It is time for "crazy increase." My super-bloom season is here!*

### The Unexpected Voice of God

Has the voice of God ever taken you by surprise? There are times when I seek the Lord and listen diligently for His voice. But on other occasions God speaks something to me seemingly out of the blue, and I then have to discern what to do with it. He has spoken to me in grocery stores, while driving my car, while in a restaurant and even in the middle of a conversation about something completely unrelated. You would expect me to be listening carefully for His voice during a time of prayer; however, one morning God caught me off guard while I was busy praying!

As I was in our morning time of prayer at Christian International, I was walking and praying in the Spirit. Suddenly I heard the Lord say, *Set the time.* I looked at my watch and it read 8:47. I looked at the clock on the wall and it read 8:42. I thought to myself humorously, *Hmmm. Is it irritating to God that the clock on the wall is running slow?* My husband is always fixing details like that—straightening pictures, resetting clock hands—so I went over to "set the time."

When I did I noticed that there was a logo in the middle of the clock and under that were the words *Established 1847.* It was 8:47, and I was setting the time on a clock that read 1847. Seemed to me God was up to something!

As I continued to walk and pray I had a couple of thoughts. First, I recognized that we are living in a "set time" of favor. In Psalm 102:13 the psalmist declares of God: "You will arise and have mercy on Zion; for the time to favor her, yes, the set time has come."

I was pondering the thought that this might be a strategic time to draw on the favor of the Lord, not only for personal advancement and blessings but also for the divine purposes of heaven being worked in our churches and in our nations. Scripturally, whenever favor shows up, everything changes. When God gave Israel favor in the sight of the Egyptians, for instance, everything changed. They were released from bondage and given great wealth, which launched them into a new season to move forward and be established. We are in such a time right now individually, corporately and in our nations.

Second, I recognized that the clock on the wall was running behind time and that the movement of the hand forward was a sign that God was catching us up with His timetable. For every instance in which there has been delay, resistance, hindrance, distraction or any other impediment to staying with God's timetable, God is now initiating the work to catch us up and put us right in the middle of His plan. This applies to personal areas of breakthrough as well as those of our churches and nations—meaning we can advance past places we may have been bogged down or gotten off course.

I was flooded with these thoughts as I continued earnestly to pray in the Spirit. Suddenly, the Lord said to me again, *Set the time.* When He repeated Himself, I realized I was not getting the full impact of what He was saying. So I began looking up every Scripture that had chapter and verse of 8:47 to see if I could further discern His message. I found that in all the Bible there are only three verses that apply.

The first and only Old Testament reference is 1 Kings 8:47, where Solomon was dedicating the Temple. He was appealing to the Lord and asking that if the nation ever faced a time when because of their sin they were taken into captivity but then recognized their wrongdoing, repented and turned their hearts back to Him, then would God heal them and restore them. Wow! They could actually set the time for their deliverance by positioning themselves properly before heaven through repentance in order to receive freedom and restoration. We are in such a time right now.

The second 8:47 verse is in the gospel of John. Here Jesus was speaking to the crowds and said that the person who is of God will hear the words of God. This is an emphasis on how imperative it is for us to hear God's voice in order to change our world.

But it was the third 8:47 verse that resonated with me in relation to working with God to "set the time"—and it has to do with receiving a miracle. It is Luke 8:47, the story of the woman who had an issue of blood. She pressed through the crowd desperately to lay hold of the hem of Jesus' garment. When she reached out and touched Him, full of faith and expectation, Jesus stopped and said, "Who touched Me?"

His disciples replied, "Lord, many are touching You. . . . We are in a crowd!"

But Jesus said, "No, someone touched Me purposely because I felt virtue/power go out of Me"—and Luke 8:47 says that her purposeful touch was the moment when the woman was immediately made whole.

She set the time for her own healing!

As I discussed this with the people I was praying with that morning, it became clear that this story was part of the heart of what God was saying. Most of the time when Jesus was healing people He was doing that which He saw the Father doing. But in this instance it was not Jesus who "set the time" for this woman's miracle; rather, the woman "set the time" through her faith, desperation and determination.

Many times when we are believing for a miracle we position ourselves and are waiting on God when, in fact, God is waiting on us to activate our faith and "set the time" for the release of the supernatural turnaround.

We see this principle in the story of the very first miracle Jesus ever performed, which was at a wedding in Cana. Mary, Jesus' mother, came to Him with her crisis: The bride and groom had run out of wine to serve the wedding guests.

Jesus replied to His mother, "Woman, what does that have to do with Me? My hour (or My time) has not yet come." Jesus was telling her, "It is not time yet for Me to do miracles."

Yet the very next verse records Mary telling the servants, "Whatever He says to you, do it!" (see John 2:1–5).

I suspect that there was more to the conversation between them. I envision that when Jesus said, "Mom, it's not time yet for Me to display My miracle power," Mary might have answered, "Listen, Jesus! I am Your mother, and You will do this for me!"

In other words, Jesus said it was not time yet, but Mary could have set the time by putting a demand on the anointing she knew He carried. She reached into the future and pulled it into the *now*.

*Now* is the set time of favor for the people of God. In the words of Smith Wigglesworth, "If the Spirit doesn't move me, then I move the Spirit."[4] Now is the time for us to "set the time" and put a demand on the anointing made available by God to release miracles of provision, turnaround and healing. Pull your future miracle into the *now* by activating your faith and pressing into His presence as never before.

## YOUR DECLARATION

*I put a demand on the anointing of God and set the time for my miracle. I am not waiting on God; He has been waiting on me. I activate my faith and recognize that Jesus has already paid the price for my miracle—physical, financial, etc.—for me and for my family. I declare that it is my turnaround season. I reach into my future and pull it into the now. I will not be stuck in a "someday" mentality that believes "someday God will bless me" or "someday God will move for me." No, I shake myself free from the "someday" mentality and stir up my heart and mind to "set the time" for faith now. I declare this in the mighty name of Jesus.*

## YOUR ACTIVATION

Identify how God speaks to you most often. Now think of a time when He said something specific to you that stirred your heart. Write that into a declaration that will enable you to come into agreement with what God has said and speak it out loud.

# The Prophet's Reward

He who receives a prophet in the name of a prophet shall
receive a prophet's reward.

Matthew 10:41

One day as I was praying I saw a vision of an ancient medieval
gate that was chained and firmly locked up. I knew that the
locked gate was not consistent with the Scripture that God
had spoken to me earlier in which Paul declared, "A wide door
of opportunity for effectual [service] has opened to me [there,
a great and promising one], and [there are] many adversaries"
(1 Corinthians 16:9 AMPC).

As I watched the vision unfold I saw a huge battering ram
begin to slam against the locked gate, shattering the chains,
crushing the lock and destroying even the hinges, causing the
gate to fall down flat and giving full access to all that was on

the other side. The most interesting part of the vision, besides the amazing visuals of breakthrough, was that written on the battering ram were the words *Prophet's Reward.*

Jesus spoke about this in Matthew 10:40–41:

> "He who receives you receives Me, and he who receives Me receives Him who sent Me. He who receives a prophet in the name of a prophet shall receive a prophet's reward. And he who receives a righteous man in the name of a righteous man shall receive a righteous man's reward."

It is very interesting that two different words are translated as "receive" in this passage. The first one is in the phrase *if you receive a prophet.* This is the Greek word *dechomai*, which means "to accept, to approve, to take hold of, to receive favorably, to give ear to, to embrace, to make one's own, not to reject, to take upon one's self, to endure, to bring into one's family, to bring up, educate and instruct, not to refuse friendship with" (*Strong's, Thayer's* 1209).

*Dechomai* is a picture of embracing something with your whole heart. It is the picture of a big hug. This is what we must do with Christ, the Prophet, in our lives. To receive Him is to receive the Father. But it also speaks of embracing the voice that will bring blessing to our lives. I believe this is where the prophetic movement has been for the past several decades. We have been receiving the ministry gift of the prophet, embracing the word of the Lord, bringing it into our lives, our homes, our churches and even into the public square. We have been educating and training up others in the Body of Christ to hear the voice of God and be empowered.

The second word translated as "receive" is completely different. The phrase *you shall receive a prophet's reward* uses the Greek word *lambanó*, which means "to take hold of, to seize for one's self, to take what is yours and make it your own, to take possession of, to apprehend, to reach after, to strive to obtain, to take back" (*Strong's, Thayer's* 2983). This word indicates an aggressive, active, almost violent alignment with heaven through acts of cooperating faith. Rather than the image of an embracing hug, this word shows us grabbing hold of something in the supernatural realm and pulling it forcefully into the realm of our reality. Wow!

The word *reward* (*misthos*) means "pay received for service or work, rewards that God bestows for good deeds and endeavors" (*Strong's, Thayer's* 3408). This is not a gift but rather compensation for those who have clung to a word, hoping against hope that what God says is true above all circumstances. God is a rewarder of those who diligently seek Him and believe His voice (see Hebrews 11:6).

When I saw the words *Prophet's Reward* written on the giant battering ram, it was slamming against that huge locked gate. As I watched and saw the gate fall down flat, I knew that the anointing of the "prophet's reward" was going to open tremendous opportunities for the Kingdom of God to advance.

Gates of influence are opening. Gates of opportunity and favor are being unlocked. Those who have received prophetic promises from God and those who operate and function in prophetic ministry will experience one of the greatest seasons of honor, advancement, promotion and favor as we align and actively participate with all God has said.

### Now Is the Time!

If you have been around prophetic meetings you have probably heard the term *prophet's reward*. So why would the Lord be emphasizing this as a tool for breakthrough? The year I had this vision marked thirty years from the time the prophetic movement was rebirthed—meaning the time when God began to reestablish the office of the prophet and the gift of prophecy. Prior to that rebirthing, there were few places in the earth experiencing dreams, visions, angelic visitations and prophetic revelation on a regular basis.

That year, however, at Christian International (as well as several other places) we experienced a new dimension of the Holy Spirit that released the power and anointing of the voice of God to all who had a heart to receive. We recognized that God was raising up a company of prophets and prophetic people who could communicate His heart, will and mind. Today, it is widely accepted throughout Christianity that God is still speaking to His people and through His people, and that as we hear God's voice it can change our world.

The fact that God was emphasizing the "prophet's reward" in the thirtieth year meant we were transitioning into a new era of the prophetic in the Body of Christ. Biblically the number thirty signifies promotion into a new season of success. This is a new era of authority and blessing for prophetic ministry and for seeing the prophesied word come to pass, and we are all now living in it. This is a launching season: Jesus was launched into His earthly ministry at the age of thirty accompanied by signs, wonders, miracles, authority, power over demons and a heart to demonstrate that the Kingdom of God had come.

Thirty is a very important number in Jewish culture. The Talmud says, "At thirty is the peak of strength."[1] It is considered to be the year of maturity for leadership, the time when a person reaches physical and mental maturity and can handle responsibility well. It is also a year of transition into the fullness of one's calling.[2] The Old Testament names several of these. Priests were dedicated to service at age thirty—*intercession* (see Numbers 4:3). Ezekiel was called as a prophet at age thirty—*prophecy* (see Ezekiel 1:1). When a young man reached the age of thirty, a Jewish father would announce to the world that his son would be the inheritor of all he had promised him, including his business: *the marketplace*.[3]

This is the main reason God waited until Jesus was thirty years old before releasing Him into His earthly ministry. Jesus' baptism was just such an announcement, when the Father proclaimed, "This is My beloved Son in whom I am well pleased." It was time for Jesus to inherit all the Father had promised Him. It was time to run His Father's business.

As we recognize that we have now crossed that spiritual threshold into breakthrough, get ready to be mantled for a new level of authority in prophetic ministry.

## A Time of Prophetic Fulfillment

The age of thirty is also linked to fulfillment of prophetic destiny, overcoming and rulership. Joseph came out of prison and had his prophetic dream fulfilled when he became a ruler in Egypt at the age of thirty. David saw the prophecy about him fulfilled when he was anointed king of Judah at Hebron at the age of thirty. Jesus was thirty when He was baptized and the Holy Spirit came upon Him and anointed Him to fulfill His prophesied destiny. All the difficulties these men went through, leading up to their times of success, were worth it when they saw everything God had promised come to pass. The "prophet's reward" launches us into similar times of fruition, when our season of testing and preparation is complete and we enter an appointed time of grace and fulfillment; we step into our positions to rule and legislate for the Kingdom of God in the earth.

The number thirty also signifies prosperity and posterity (meaning blessings for the generations). In Judges 10:4 we read that one of the judges, Jair, had thirty sons. He gave each of them a horse and a city!

So you see, when I had that vision it marked a new era of prophetic ministry. All that had gone before was actually only preparatory to what would come next. In the early days the prophetic was met with skepticism and resistance; now there is honor and excitement to hear the word of the Lord. And in this new era we will see increasing signs and wonders accompanying the words spoken. The voice of God is being heard in our churches and being drawn on in the business world. Many local and national governmental officials long to hear answers from the heart of God. As these leaders receive and honor prophetic ministry and align themselves with prophetic anointing, they have the capacity to bring their cities—or even nations—into the "prophet's reward" of blessing and breakthrough. One of the new things to watch for is how effectively prophets and prophetic ministry cross into the mainstream of culture, not just the mainstream of the Church. Secular leaders will become increasingly open to hearing what God is saying, even those who do not know Him yet.

The Lord is saying that it is time for each of us to receive the "prophet's reward." Whether you were part of what God did in the past or you are brand new to the movement, your reward is the same. During this new era we should all expect greater anointing to commission God's people for leadership, ministry, fulfillment of prophetic destiny and rulership, blessings of prosperity upon ourselves and the coming generations, greater revelation and greater miracles, signs and wonders than ever before.

### So, What Is the "Prophet's Reward"?

When I asked the Lord for understanding of what a "prophet's reward" actually is, my first thought from Him was, *It's the way I rewarded My prophets!*

Simple, right? Moses was a prophet, and he saw God face-to-face. Samuel was a prophet, and not one of his words fell to the ground. David was a prophet, and he was called a man after God's own heart. Elijah was a prophet, and he called down fire from heaven. Elisha was a prophet, and he used the double-portion mantle to confront death in many forms, including to liberate cities from barrenness and famine. Jesus was a prophet who brought heaven down to earth. God wants to reward us in much the same way. He wants to bring us into face-to-face encounters and release authority to us that can shift heaven and change earth.

There are numerous examples in Scripture of people being blessed, rewarded and advanced because they received a prophet or a prophetic message. In all these examples we find that receiving the prophet or prophetic word was not a passive response—simply hearing a word and hoping something good would happen as a result. Rather, the response of the people to the prophetic required active alignment, an expectant attitude and corresponding action. The "prophet's reward" released the promise from the Lord but also empowered the hearer with the anointing that was upon the prophet or prophetic minister. The "prophet's reward" released rapid fulfillment of the things God had promised.

In most of the instances below, the prophecy was fulfilled almost instantly, without delay. The "prophet's reward" accelerates the process of divine fulfillment.

### 1. The Reward That Money Cannot Buy

*Prophets release the miraculous.* The story of the Shunammite woman is probably one of the best examples of receiving a "prophet's reward" in all of Scripture. In 2 Kings 4 we meet this woman who was wealthy, but had no child. Initially she invited the prophet Elisha for meals when he passed through her town, but then she actually had an upper room built for him to stay in. This shows the *dechomai* meaning of *receive*; she welcomed him in.

Each of us needs to be challenged to build a room in our lives and in our hearts for the word of the Lord to indwell. Rather than just occasionally receiving "a word" we receive the abiding voice of God. When this woman welcomed the prophet to reside with her and her husband, she was welcoming anointing in her home (in her life) knowing that that anointing would bring blessing. So rather than just provide the prophet with food when he came to town, she built a room for him. It would serve as a place for the prophetic voice of God, as well as for God's presence and power.

God is asking each one of us to *dechomai* the prophetic anointing by building a place in our lives, homes, businesses, churches and nations for the voice of God. We must build a place in which God's prophetic voice and His presence can activate the "prophet's reward."

After the prophet moved in, he wanted to bring the "prophet's reward" into her life by blessing her. When he asked what she needed, she said she did not need anything. Elisha learned, however, that she did not have an heir. He spoke a prophecy that the following year she would bear a son. The woman was so full of disappointment and grief from her years of barrenness that her initial reaction was not one of faith but rather one signifying, "Don't mess with me, prophet!" Nevertheless, the next year she had a son.

The Shunammite had honored the gift within the prophet by welcoming him; she had made a place for the prophetic anointing in her life by building a place for the prophet to dwell; and she received a miracle that money could not buy.

Her story tells us further that one of the beautiful things about a "prophet's reward" is that the miraculous is not a one-time blessing; the anointing continues through the years.

When the boy was older he was out in the field with his father and suddenly complained of pain in his head. A servant took the boy to his mother, and there he died. The Shunammite, drawing on the "prophet's reward" anointing, ran to get the prophet to raise her son back to life. She was no longer operating in the *dechomai* aspect of *receive*, welcoming a prophet. Now, when she needed a miracle, she moved into *lambanó*, aggressively going after the anointing of prophetic breakthrough. Her heir was given back to her; everything the enemy robbed was returned.

This theme continues in 2 Kings 8. Elisha advised the Shunammite to go with her family and live somewhere else because the Lord had decreed a famine. She was gone seven years and then returned to make an appeal for her house and her land. The king was literally hearing the story from Elisha's servant of how Elisha had raised the boy back to life when she entered. The servant said, "Look! Here is the woman and her son."

The "prophet's reward" set her up with anointing for favor to be in the right place at the right time. The king gave her back not only her land but all the proceeds from the land that should have been hers for the previous seven years. The "prophet's reward" will bring restoration of all that has been lost or stolen. It is a blessing that keeps on giving. In this era of the "prophet's reward" God will make sure you are in the right place at the right time to receive your miracle and to have influence for His Kingdom.

Not only will God bless those who have made room in their personal lives for His voice, but He will see that blessings come upon churches and businesses that have made a place for the prophetic within the organization's structure. Have you given

God's voice a place to move and speak wherever you are? If so, then you will see the Shunammite blessing of the "prophet's reward"; growth and increase will be the result. God will bring you the miracle you need that money cannot buy.

### 2. The Reward of Provision

*Prophets release provision.* In 1 Kings 17 we read that Elisha's mentor, the prophet Elijah, received a word from God to go to a widow in Zarephath to be fed during a time of famine. When he got there he found the woman gathering sticks by the city gate, preparing to fix her last meal for her and her son before dying of starvation. He asked her for water, then for bread, and she replied that she had only a tiny bit of flour and oil left.

He asked her to go fix him a small cake because he knew God had sent him to this widow to break the back of lack in her life. Then he gave her a promise that if she did this, the bin of flour would not be empty and the oil would not run dry. The widow received his prophetic word and fed him, and then she and her household ate for many days. The prophet was blessed with food—and also with the provision of an upper room—and the woman received the "prophet's reward" of unlimited supply for her and her whole household as long as she had need. Not only that, but sometime later her son became ill and died. The prophet stayed in covenant with her and raised him back to life.

It is time to see the "prophet's reward" of unlimited supply and resurrection life manifested—not just for survival but for advancement of the Kingdom endeavors God has challenged us with.

### 3. The Reward of Posterity

*Prophets bring generational continuity.* As we saw in the previous story, not only did the widow experience provision for her household through the "prophet's reward," but when her son died, the prophet brought him back to life. Likewise, the "prophet's reward" as it relates to posterity is seen in 2 Kings 4.

A prophet died and left his wife in debt. Her two boys were about to be taken as slaves by the creditor. The prophet Elisha told the woman to take the small amount of oil she had, go gather as many vessels as she could, and begin to pour the oil into them. Her obedience to the word resulted in a "prophet's reward" of supernatural multiplication of oil, which enabled her to pay the debt and set her children free. She worked with the word of the Lord through the prophet to see her future generations free and blessed.

We also see an example of the "prophet's reward" and generational synergy in the ministries of Elijah and Elisha themselves. Elijah prophesied to Elisha, and Elisha responded by going after Elijah wholeheartedly until he received the double-portion blessing. The double-portion anointing and the "prophet's reward" are synonymous. It is time to receive this fresh mantle on your life, family, ministry and business.

### 4. The Reward of New Beginnings

*Prophets declare new things and reformation.* Truthfully, I think everyone of us can benefit from a fresh start, renewed vision and anticipation of a new adventure. Isaiah 42:9 says, "Behold, the former things have come to pass, and new things I declare; before they spring forth I tell you of them." This is prophetic function: to declare what God is doing before it even happens. Isaiah 43:19 says, "Behold, I will do a new thing, now it shall spring forth; shall you not know it?" This season will be full of new things as reformation aligns God's people to proper heart-positioning and proper function so the Church can thrive as Christ intended.

### 5. The Reward of Breakthrough

*Prophets bring breakthrough.* David was Jesse's eighth son, and he ushered in a new era for Israel when he received a prophetic word from Samuel that he would be king. David believed that word, received it and then acted on it by stepping up to face Goliath. The "prophet's reward" released vision, courage and a prophetic edge for David; this anointing brought Goliath down.

This will be an era to see Goliaths fall. Goliath systems. Goliaths of intimidation. Goliaths of impossibility. The "prophet's reward" releases the ability to do things that have been impossible before. It is a breaker anointing that brings down spiritual foes. This is a record-breaking time. Things that have never been achieved before will come into breakthrough. Things stagnated or stalemated in previous years will break open through the word of the Lord.

### 6. The Reward of Opportunity and Favor

*Prophets release favor and open doors of opportunity.* The prophet Moses stood before the throne of Pharaoh and spoke these words from the Lord: "Let My people go." When Pharaoh finally relented, God released favor for His people among the Egyptians (see Exodus 12:36).

In the Hebraic alphabet the number eight is drawn as a picture of a gate or a door. Remember my vision of the battering ram inscribed with the words *Prophet's Reward* pounding against a giant gate. Gates were places of government and authority. Kings issued decrees from the city gates. Prophets prophesied from the gates. Jesus raised the dead in the gate. Elijah encountered the widow of Zarephath in the gate. The apostles healed the lame man in the gate. Jesus identified Himself as the door. In the book of Revelation He says that

He has the key of David, and opens so that no one can shut and shuts so that no one can open (see Revelation 3:7). Expect doors of favor and access that have been shut to you in the past to be open to you for your future.

Paul wrote that "a wide door for effective work has opened to me, and there are many adversaries" (1 Corinthians 16:9 ESV). I believe that even as we embrace the prophetic words God is releasing in this season and as we see unprecedented times of open doors, we also may have to contend with adversaries. But take heart and have no fear. I heard the Lord say, *Your opposition will become your opportunity.* When David faced Goliath and defeated him, he was rewarded with promotion: He was given the king's daughter's hand in marriage and moved into the palace. The opposition became his opportunity. In the same way, your adversaries will lead to your advantage. Your trial and trouble will become your triumph.

I believe this season will be characterized by gates, Goliaths and glory. Go through the gates, defeat your Goliaths and then step into His glory.

### 7. The Reward That Heaven Will Fight For You

*Prophets release heaven's angel armies.* We see several times in Scripture that when a prophetic word is released and the people of God position themselves in agreement with that word, then heaven intervenes supernaturally in their battles.

In Judges 4–5 we read that Deborah released a prophetic word regarding oppression from the Canaanites. A military contingent responded by going to the prophetically indicated place by the River Kishon. *Kishon* comes from a root word *qush* meaning "to set a trap or lay a snare for the enemy" (*Strong's* 6983). This is exactly what happened as part of the "prophet's reward." When the enemy showed up to fight God's people, He caused torrential rain to fall, flooding the riverbed. Those Canaanites who did not die by the sword were washed away: The heavens fought for Israel (see Judges 5:20–21).

In another battle described in 2 Chronicles 20, Jehoshaphat, a great reformer and righteous king, learned of a vast army coming against him. He called the people to fast and seek the Lord during which time the Spirit of the Lord came upon Jahaziel, who prophesied that they would not need to fight in the battle for "the battle is the Lord's."

As a response to this prophetic word, Jehoshaphat sent worshipers out in front of the army singing, "Praise the Lord for His mercy endures forever." Once the men of Judah reached the enemy, they discovered that the soldiers had turned on one another and wiped each other out. Heaven got involved and fought for them.

Part of our "prophet's reward" is that God will cause His angels to fight for us. Hebrews 1:14 says that God sends His angels to assist those who are to inherit salvation. In the book of Acts we read multiple times that angels intervened to deliver the apostles and position them to advance the Gospel of the Kingdom. This is part of our reward for receiving God's prophetic voice. Send down Your mighty ones, O God!

### 8. The Reward of Nation-Changing

*Prophets change cities and nations.* Jeremiah was tasked as a prophet to the nations to root up, tear down, throw down, destroy and also to build and plant. The prophetic anointing has the ability to shift an atmosphere over a territory, which can result in changes in government, business and economy, and even break the territory open for revival. We see this demonstrated in 2 Kings 2 after Elisha received the double-portion mantle from Elijah. The first thing he did was go to Jericho and break the curse of death and barrenness off the city. The city was forever changed by the word of the prophet; the city that received him received the prophet's reward.

The "prophet's reward" has been made available now more than ever. We are shifting into a new anointing to *lambanó* all the purposes of God. It is time for breakthrough. It is time to lay hold. It is time for fulfillment and maturity. It is time for release. It is time to step proactively into your "prophet's reward." Align with all that God has charged you with, embrace the prophetic anointing that God is releasing to you and receive your prophet's reward!

## YOUR DECLARATION

*I am living in the era of the "prophet's reward." I will* dechomai, *embrace, the word of the Lord and I will* lambanó, *seize and take possession of, all my prophetic promises. As I listen for God's voice, I do not receive just a word but an anointing as well, to do signs, wonders and miracles. I receive the miracle I need that money cannot buy (name it here). I receive supernatural provision, blessings on my generations and opportunities for new beginnings. I receive the anointing for breakthrough and will see Goliaths fall. I receive opportunity and favor, for there is a wide door open before me for effectual ministry. Though there will be adversaries, I will always prevail, for heaven will fight for me. I will be a nation-changer carrying revival everywhere I go. I lay hold of the "prophet's reward" and step into my new era.*

## YOUR ACTIVATION

How have you received (*dechomai*: embraced, welcomed, accepted, given ear to) prophetic words in the past? Have you written the words down, meditated on them, decreed promises from them? Write down several things God has promised you prophetically.

Now it is time to *lambanó* those prophetic promises (to seize them, take possession of them, to take hold of them, to strive to obtain them). Write down some ways you can actively align with these promises through acts of cooperating faith.

# A Quantum Leap Season

"I foretold the former things long ago, my mouth announced them and I made them known; then suddenly I acted, and they came to pass."

Isaiah 48:3 NIV1984

Once, as I was getting ready to minister at a local business leaders' meeting, I heard the Lord say distinctly that we are entering a time of "quantum leap" anointing. I had of course heard the term *quantum leap* before, but I did not understand how it related to what God desired to do in and through His Church.

*Quantum leap* is defined as a "sudden and significant change or increase; something sudden, spectacular and vitally important,[1] a sudden highly significant advance or breakthrough."[2] Am I ever ready for this!

The man who was leading the meeting had heard the Lord call him to run for mayor of his city. Several months earlier he had filed all the necessary paperwork to get his name on the ballot. But that morning, as God declared a "quantum leap" anointing, the man got a phone call from the supervisor of elections telling him that no one had filed papers to run as his opponent. Suddenly, he was going to become mayor of the city—no campaigning, no need to spend money, no election—he was elected mayor without any opposition. It was definitely a "quantum leap" moment for him as he experienced a sudden and significant advance.

With this great confirmation in front of me I began to do further research on the topic of the quantum leap. I am by no means a quantum physicist, but I spoke with several people who are as I attempted to research this complex science. I found that people who practice Eastern Mysticism and New Age spirituality have hijacked this science with lots of bizarre theories. So I have attempted to stick closely to the science of quantum mechanics as we explore what it could mean for us to be moving into a "quantum leap" season.

The simplest way to describe quantum science is as a study of energy at the subatomic level, the smallest particles in existence. A *quantum leap* is described as an abrupt movement of an electron from one radiant energy level to another with no smooth transition—no "in between." An electron will build up energy, accelerate or become "excited," spinning around with energy, then will suddenly jump or leap to another level to orbit another nucleus of an atom. As it does, the photons emit a burst of light. It goes from point *A* to point *B* instantly. Once it makes this jump, it finds a place of stabilizing and then begins to build energy once more to work up to the next leap to the next level.[3] In a quantum leap—*bam!* Everything changes.

For the Church, it defines a "suddenly" season filled with light, energy and power that redefines our present and our future.

## "Quantum Leap" Freedom

This is what happens when we have an encounter with Jesus—*bam!* Everything changes. Like the children of Israel coming out of Egypt after Passover—*bam!* One minute they are slaves, the next moment they are declared free. When we encounter Jesus, our Passover Lamb—*bam!* A lifetime of slavery, bondage, addiction, fear, sin is destroyed in a moment. We leap out of the kingdom of darkness into the Kingdom of God's Son—the Kingdom of Light. This is a time of "quantum leap" freedom as God's people experience and appropriate the power of the cross on a whole new level.

One moment you are sick then—*bam!* You are suddenly healed.

One moment you are bound by darkness and oppression then—*bam!* The light of God's love makes you free, full of joy, full of light.

One moment you are poor with nothing working for you then—*bam!* God turns things around releasing His divine favor and opening new doors of opportunity and blessing.

It is time for God's people to build up excitement and energy by releasing our faith, dreaming bigger dreams and praying in the Holy Spirit then—*bam!*—leaping from glory to glory, from faith to faith and from strength to strength. This will be a time of exponential increase for the Body of Christ.

## The Quantum Kingdom

Three days after the Lord spoke to me about a time of "quantum leap" anointing, I had an early flight to travel to speak at a conference. I am not an early morning person, so I am not very talkative on these flights. The man seated next to me, however, was obviously a morning person. He was bright and cheerful and wanted to talk.

Eventually, when I realized I was not going to be able to sleep, I asked him, "So what do you do for a living?"

To which the man replied, "I teach quantum physics at a university."

I said, "Really? Wow! Do I have some questions for you!"

I knew this was a divine appointment. He talked with me about the quantum realm and how the study of quantum physics is actually causing some scientists to acknowledge there has to be a Creator, or at least some sort of intelligent design.[4]

He explained that quantum physicists have found that there are two realms of reality. One is called the present realm, which can be described as the realm of the life we are living. The second is the quantum realm, where scientists say anything is possible. It is described as a reality in which there is "infinite possibility" and "unlimited potential."

I believe this indicates that scientists are seeing into the reality of the realm Jesus called the Kingdom of God. Everything He did demonstrated this quantum realm of the Kingdom. Each time He healed someone of sickness or disease, He was demonstrating this realm of infinite possibility. When He walked on water, He was demonstrating that this present realm of existence is subjugated to this other supernatural realm. When He was transfigured, He was manifesting the unseen realm of quantum Kingdom glory in the midst of the earth realm. Everything He did showed that the Kingdom of God is actually right here among us, available to us, a supernatural realm in which anything is possible.

In Acts 8 we see Philip experiencing this quantum realm and making a quantum leap. One minute he is baptizing the Ethiopian eunuch and the next moment—*bam!* He is translated instantly from one location to another—from the middle of a desert to the middle of the city of Azotus. Philip entered the quantum realm of "infinite possibility," thus demonstrating the limitless power of the Kingdom of God.

### "Quantum Leap" Power

Similarly, the disciples experienced "quantum leap" power and anointing on the Day of Pentecost. After Jesus had ascended to heaven and they had gathered together for ten days, suddenly—*bam!* The room they were in was filled with a sound of a rushing mighty wind, and they were all baptized with the Holy Ghost and fire. They were given power from on high to go out and work miracles, cast out demons and preach the Gospel of the Kingdom with boldness. In one instant they were transformed.

This is similar to but much more powerful than what occurred when Elisha received the double-portion mantle from Elijah. Prior to that time Elisha had never done one miracle then—*bam!* From that moment forward he demonstrated God's transforming power everywhere he went. He experienced the "quantum leap" anointing and power of God.

In this season God's people must cry out as Elisha did, "Please let a double portion of your Spirit be upon me" (2 Kings 2:9). In response, God is giving His people a new mantle for a new day. It is a double-portion mantle—but we must realize that what we have received with the infilling of the Holy Spirit is far more powerful than the mantle Elijah passed to Elisha. It carries the very anointing of Christ to set people, nations and generations free.

We are living in a time of favor from heaven where signs, wonders and miracles will become widespread—not only within our churches but in the marketplace as well, as believers begin to awaken and arise to the transforming power of God that is within them.

I had a dream in which I pulled my car up to a garage that offered oil changes for vehicles. There was a sign in the window that said: "Change Your Oil. It Will Change Your Life!" I believe this is what the Lord is saying to His Church—we need an oil change. Psalm 92:10 encourages us to embrace this. It says, "I have been anointed with fresh oil." There is a "fresh oil" anointing for those who are pressing into His presence and His promises.

## "Quantum Leap" Awakening

God has set us up for a "quantum leap" season of the move of His Spirit into a time of great awakening. Revivals here and there will no longer suffice. We need an awakening. I believe an awakening is an epidemic revival. The word *epidemic* means "affecting many people at the same time, spreading from person to person in a location where something is not prevalent, a rapid spread or increase in something making it widespread."[5] We need epidemic revival in our nations today.

Remember, in a quantum leap the electrons build up energy and become jittery or "excited." Scientists actually use this word to describe it. God is releasing supernatural miracles and favor to His people so we can become excited again. Momentum is building in the Spirit. We need to set our hearts to take all the limits off of God.

I heard the Lord say that we have entered a time when He is going to make Himself real in spectacular ways. His purpose in this is to restore hope to the Church so the Church can then restore hope to the world. Scripture empowers us with these words:

> Now may God, the inspiration and fountain of hope, fill you to overflowing with uncontainable joy and perfect peace as you trust in him. And may the power of the Holy Spirit continually surround your life with his super-abundance until you radiate with hope!
>
> Romans 15:13 TPT

We will encounter the God of hope in a new and powerful way, and as we are strengthened and encouraged so, too, we can show the God of hope, Jesus, to the world.

## "Quantum Leap" Provision

We had a couple in our church whose company was seriously affected by an economic downturn. They had a contract with the state for $1.5 million, which got cancelled due to the recession. They were living on savings and thought perhaps the whole company would need to close its doors.

One Sunday they heard me preach a message about the spirit of robbery, based on Exodus 22:7: If caught, a thief must restore double. They looked at each other and said, "We have been robbed!" So the next week they reapplied for their contract with the state, wrote a decree, sowed an offering and had us pray over all of it. I felt led by the Lord to say to them that the government would tell them no first before saying yes.

The next week they got a call from the governor's office saying that their application for funding was being denied. They were told they could apply again the following year.

After the call, they got excited saying, "They told us no; next they are going to tell us yes!" They believed and decreed the prophetic word.

Two days later they got another call from the governor's office. The individual said, "Well, it seems that your application for funding has been approved. But as we looked into your file we found you should never have been defunded in the first place. So, we are going to restore last year's funding of one-and-a-half-million dollars, but then double this year's funding to three million. Your company should be receiving a check for four-and-a-half-million dollars in the next couple of weeks."

And the story does not end there! The couple got subsequent phone calls from offices of both the governor and the senate regarding funding for their company, expressing the desire to accelerate their project. Their annual funding was increased from $3 million, to $9 million, to $17 million, to $25 million. All because they decided not to take no as their final answer.

This is quantum provision. God shifts us from scarcity to abundance in one giant leap in our areas of need. In the realm of finances, for example, as we sow financial seeds we should expect a "quantum leap" release into our own finances. We have many testimonies of financial miracles in which debt has been suddenly cancelled, properties have sold, new contracts have been signed. Expansion, blessing and prosperity are breaking out in the lives of many.

### "Quantum Leap" Harvest

To further demonstrate the concept of the "quantum leap" anointing that takes place in a "suddenly" season allow me to relate the story of Chinese bamboo. It is a costly, precious wood grown in certain places in China. The first year the farmer plows his field and prepares the ground for the bamboo seed. He then digs small holes for each seed and plants the crop. He waters it, fertilizes it and weeds it, carefully watching over the ground in which his crop is growing.

At the end of the first year when he surveys the progress of growth, he sees nothing—no sign of life, no tender shoot, nothing. In the second year he waters, weeds, fertilizes and tends his field; but again, at the end of that year . . . nothing. By the end of the third growing season a small shoot pushes its way above the soil. It achieves only about three inches of growth. So far it averages one inch per year. That is not exactly impressive. By the end of the fourth year of growth the plant measures a little over a foot tall.

But then in the fifth year of growth the bamboo shoot hits a growing season, which lasts four months. During those four months the bamboo that the farmer has tended for five years suddenly shoots up eighty feet. There are days in which the bamboo actually grows three or four feet in a single day. *Suddenly!*[6]

I think we all have come to realize that God's "suddenlies" do not always happen suddenly. But we are now in a "quantum leap" season where we will see those things—things we have prayed for, decreed, quoted Scriptures for, prophesied and warred good warfare for—suddenly come to pass. This is a now season. We cannot be discouraged or disappointed by the previous years of looking out over our planted fields of promise and seeing no visible results of our labor. Because suddenly—*bam!*

It is the season for rapid growth, fulfillment and harvest. It is time to experience the quantum power of the Kingdom of God. Miracles, signs and wonders are our portion as we take off the limits and arise to our potential in Christ Jesus.

Quantum glory is at hand!

## YOUR DECLARATION

*I am living in my "quantum leap" season. I will experience "suddenlies" in God, where what I have prayed for, decreed and prophesied suddenly comes to pass. I will see God's Kingdom manifested in my life as a realm of infinite possibility and unlimited potential. I will see "quantum leap" power, provision, awakening and harvest. This is my time for a giant leap forward to experience the fullness of the glory of God in my life. I declare this in Jesus' name.*

## YOUR ASSIGNMENT

Identify one area where you expect to see a "quantum leap" or "suddenly" of God that will bring you into fulfillment. Seek the Lord about how to align your life to see this fulfillment and find scriptural support for what you are expecting. Now activate your faith and make a decree.

# 10

# Declarations for Breakthrough

You are my King and my God, who decrees victories for Jacob.

Psalm 44:4 NIV

God loves to decree victory over His people. He is seated on His heavenly throne speaking decrees over the earth, longing for His people to hear His voice and begin to speak the same things in the earth realm. When we begin to speak and declare His word, breakthrough happens. He created us with power in our words that can change the course of history. When we agree with His written Word and His prophetic words to us all heaven stands at attention.

The Word of God is His voice in printed form. It is quick and powerful and sharper than a two-edged sword. It is able to save our souls. It is inspired by God. It will light our paths and give us direction. It stands forever, not changing with times or seasons. It revives us in times of trouble. It brings joy. It brings healing and deliverance. It keeps us from sin. It accomplishes God's purposes. It always brings hope.[1]

Psalm 103:20–21 declares, "Praise the LORD, you angels of his, you powerful warriors who carry out his decrees and obey his orders! Praise the LORD, all you warriors of his, you servants of his who carry out his desires!" (NET). The angel armies are standing at attention awaiting orders from the mouth of God. We must realize that God has already spoken His decrees and His orders through the Scriptures. When we declare His word—whether written or given to us prophetically—angels are mobilized.

In my book *Discernment*, I explain the following about angel armies:

> As previously noted God has armies of angels in heaven who are fighting alongside Michael for the sake of God's people. God is identified 238 times in the Old Testament by the term *Lord of hosts*. This term actually indicates that God is the Lord of the angel armies. The word *hosts* is the Hebrew word *tsaba* [*Strong's* 6635], which means "a mass of people organized for war or a campaign, an army of soldiers or warriors." God has an army of warriors organized under His command to carry out His word. One of His names is Jehovah Tsabaoth— "the Lord of the Angel Armies." When we speak and decree words from God, He activates His angel armies to carry out His commands.[2]

Since the words of God are the most powerful forces in the universe, I have written some declarations straight from the Scriptures that will bring breakthrough when spoken aloud. When we contemplate Scripture quietly in our hearts, there is power to change us within; however, when these words are spoken out loud in agreement with the voice of God, all heaven and earth are stirred to accommodate God's will. Angels arise to carry out their assignments.

## Prayer and Decree of Repentance

So often when believers begin to arise in the authority and spiritual positioning God desires, the enemy of our souls comes with his words of accusation and condemnation, attempting to undercut the power of our prayers and decrees. The answer to this is simple: prayers of repentance. Our unconfessed sin causes us to live lives full of guilt and condemnation and out of alignment with heaven. It hinders our prayers and ability to decree with power.

In the prayer Jesus taught His disciples He said, "Forgive us our debts, as we forgive our debtors. And do not lead us into temptation, but deliver us from the evil one. For Yours is the kingdom and the power and the glory forever. Amen" (Matthew 6:12–13).

Jesus paid the price for our sin, and no matter how we may try to hide from Him, He knows our hearts and the things we have done; therefore, be honest with Him. Be real with Him. Humble yourself before Him and pray this prayer with me.

### LET'S PRAY

*Heavenly Father, thank You for sending Your Son, Jesus, to pay the penalty for my sin. Thank You for Your steadfast love toward me, so that even though I choose to go my own way instead of Yours, You are always drawing me back to You with love and forgiveness. Thank You that Your Word says that when I confess my sin, You are faithful and just to forgive my sin and to cleanse me from all unrighteousness. I confess my sin before You now (be specific as the Holy Spirit leads you). I am sorry for my choices and my failures. I turn away from my sin and turn toward Your love, righteousness and grace. I ask You to remove my sin from me as far as the east is from the west. I forgive those who have sinned against me (again, be specific with your forgiveness; let go of all offense and release the individual from all judgment). I receive Your healing and freedom from pain and shame. Create in me a clean heart, Lord, and renew a right spirit within me. Do not cast me away from Your presence, and please do not take Your Holy Spirit from me. Restore to me the joy of Your salvation and uphold me by Your generous Spirit.[3] In the mighty name of Jesus I ask this. Amen.*

## YOUR DECLARATION

*I am the righteousness of God in Christ. I do not belong to the devil; I belong to Jesus. I am forgiven of all my sins, so, devil, shut your mouth! I was chosen in Jesus before the foundation of the world to be holy and without blame before God in love. I am called, chosen and faithful. I submit myself to God; I resist the devil, and he must flee. God is able to keep me from stumbling. I am established in righteousness and oppression is far from me. I am delivered from the powers of darkness and translated into the Kingdom of God's dear Son. I shake off all shame and condemnation because Christ has made me free. I am pure and holy because Christ says I am. I am strengthened with might by His Spirit in my inner man. I am an overcomer because*

*greater is He that is in me than he that is in the world.*
*No weapon formed against me has any chance of pros-*
*pering for I have found favor with God and my fellow*
*man. I decree these things in Jesus' name.*[4]

---------------- NOW DECREE THIS ----------------

*I break off every spirit of shame, guilt and condemna-*
*tion, every lie of the enemy, every spirit of intimidation*
*and fear, every spirit of depression, oppression or even*
*suicide. I submit myself to God. I resist the devil, and*
*he must flee. I stand in the power of Jesus Christ and*
*triumph over my enemies.*

### The Authority of the Believer

Jesus gave power and authority to His followers so they might
live lives of breakthrough and victory. Even in times of suffering, trial or challenge, believers are given the promise of
overcoming and living lives that demonstrate the dominion
of the Kingdom of God in the earth. This power and authority enable believers to walk in the authority Christ walked
in while in His flesh on the earth. He did every miracle, cast
out every devil and even raised the dead not because He was
God (which He was), but as a man filled with the power of
the Holy Spirit. He was demonstrating for us that we can
walk in the same power and authority as human beings filled
with God's power.

This book has discussed at length the concept of power—
the *dunamis* of God—and how we are filled with supernatural
ability to accomplish our assignments on earth. The word
*authority*, however, is the Greek word *exousia*, which speaks
of delegated authority to rule or to have influence. Rulers in

the first century were referred to as *exousia*, the authorities who held public office over a region primarily through birth or appointment.

Jesus gave His disciples this kind of legislative authority by giving them His authority. Just as those rulers were subject to Caesar, from whom they derived their limited earthly power, the authority of the believer is delegated directly from Christ Himself who was given all authority in heaven and on earth (see Matthew 28:18). Our authority comes as we are submitted to the Lord of heaven and earth. So let's stir up that authority and make some decrees!

## YOUR DECLARATION
### FOR SPIRITUAL AUTHORITY

*I am seated in heavenly places through my relationship with Christ Jesus. I do not have a spirit of fear, but am flooded with the anointing for love, power and a sound mind. I am bold and courageous. I am stepping out of my comfort zone. I have power and authority over all demons and can cure diseases. Every place the sole of my foot steps, God has given to me as an ambassador for His Kingdom. I can do the same miraculous works that Jesus did; in fact, He said I would do even greater things. The same Spirit who raised Christ from the dead lives in me and has the power to quicken mortal bodies. I can heal the sick and even raise the dead. The Spirit of the Lord is upon me and has anointed me to preach and proclaim good news to the poor, to proclaim liberty to those who are captive, to give recovery of sight to the blind and freedom to those who are oppressed. I will proclaim the time of God's favor. Nothing is impossible for me. As a matter of fact, signs and wonders are following me. I speak in new tongues; I move in miracles; I deal with demons, even Satan himself, and nothing can harm me. When I lay my hands on the sick, they are made well instantly. Whatever I bind on earth is bound in heaven; whatever I loose on earth is loosed in heaven. What I forbid is forbidden and what I allow is allowed. I am part of the* ekklesia; *therefore, the very gates of hell will not prevail against me. I am full of authority and will rule and reign with Christ, to cause His Kingdom to come and His will to be done on earth as it is in heaven. I decree this in Jesus' name.*[5]

## YOUR DECLARATION
### FOR VICTORY IN SPIRITUAL WARFARE

*Thanks be to God, who always gives me victory. I am a warrior. I am empowered for victory with Your wrap-around presence. Your power within me makes me strong. You give me victory on every side. I will exercise authority through the victory Jesus won on the cross, confronting and exposing the enemy's plans. I am able because God within me is greater than any devil from hell or any person on the earth. I will, therefore, give no opportunity to the devil and will fight the good fight of faith. I have the Holy Spirit within; therefore, I can discern any plan of the enemy or any tactic from hell. The God of peace is crushing Satan under my feet. I am strong in the Lord and the power of His might. In the name of Jesus, I have the power to tread on serpents and scorpions and over all the power of the enemy, and nothing shall hurt me. I am not weak, double-minded or fearful. I am sober-minded and vigilant, always watch-ing in the Spirit. I love people and want to see them set*

173

*free; therefore, I do not wage war with fleshly human weapons but with spiritual weapons, and I am able to pull down the strongholds of the enemy. I put on my warrior's armor. I put on my belt of truth to strengthen me as I stand in triumph. I put on holiness as my protective armor that covers my heart. I put on my shoes of peace so I will always be ready to share the blessings of the Lord with others. In every battle, I will take faith as my wrap-around shield, for it is able to extinguish the blazing arrows coming at me from the evil one. I put on my helmet of salvation that causes me to embrace the power of deliverance and protect my mind from evil thoughts and lies. Finally, I take my razor-sharp sword of the Spirit, which is the spoken word of God. I claim great victories for my family, for my nation and for the Kingdom of God. O God, bring Your breakthrough-victory! I decree this in Jesus' name.*[6]

## Your Declaration
### for Greater Prophetic Revelation

*I was created to hear the voice of the Lord. Jesus expects me to hear His voice. I will listen intentionally, and I will hear intelligently so I can discern and obey what He says. I have received the Holy Spirit; therefore, I will also receive dreams, visions and prophecy. I have the spirit of wisdom and revelation through my knowledge of Him, so my eyes are opened and I can see. I am not spiritually blind but have my eyes wide open to the things of the spiritual realm. I can discern angels and demons. I can discern what God is doing. I can discern the times. I can even discern false motives behind the actions of others so I can be warned but also pray for them. When I speak what He says it has the power to shatter the enemy. When I prophesy by revelation then healings and miracles result. I will not be shy, timid or fearful, but will boldly declare the word of the Lord. God needs my voice in the earth to release His plans, purposes and power. His words in my mouth will root things up, tear some things down and also build and plant for the Kingdom of God. I will be a voice for the Lord to my generation. I decree this in Jesus' name.*[7]

## Your Declaration
## for Protection

*I live under divine protection. I declare that my hope and trust are in the Lord, who is my refuge and fortress. I activate my faith and give no place to fear, for God is my help in time of need. The enemy cannot touch me for I am safe under the shadow of His wings. God is faithful and will strengthen and protect me from the evil one. God will never leave me or forsake me. He always answers me in my time of trouble. He is Jehovah Jireh, my Provider; Jehovah Rapha, my Healer; and Jehovah Shalom, my Peace. He keeps me safe from evil and will not allow any sickness to come near my home. He places angels around me and my family to keep us safe from all harm. The angels have special orders from God to protect and defend me. God gives me peace in the midst of my storm. Because I carry the dunamis of the Living God inside me, the Holy Spirit places a force field around me keeping me safe, strong and healthy in my body, soul and spirit. I am blessed and not cursed! I am a blessing and strength to others in their times of need. I am a source of God's light and life and bring glory to the Lord in all I say and do. I agree with God's Word that this will be my time of victory, peace and increase. I decree this in Jesus' mighty name.*[8]

<h2 style="text-align:center">YOUR DECLARATION<br>FOR BLESSING AND PROSPERITY</h2>

*I am blessed and highly favored of the Lord. God created me to be blessed so I can be a blessing. He makes all I do prosper in my hand. I have the power to create wealth to establish His covenant. God loves me, blesses me and multiplies for me abundantly. His word makes my way prosperous and makes me abundantly successful. He sends angels before me to prosper me in my journey. I believe God's prophets, and I prosper. The Lord blesses me and His favor is around me like a shield. Because I seek the Lord, I do not lack any good thing. He has brought me to a wealthy place, and wealth and riches are in my house. Peace is within my walls, and prosperity is in my home. I honor the Lord with my giving, so my barns are filled with plenty and my vats are bursting forth with new wine. I am generous and I prosper; I refresh others, and I myself am refreshed. Instead of shame I receive the double portion of blessing. Anything the thief has stolen from me must be given back at least double. I receive double for my trouble. I break the power of poverty, lack and limitation, and I repent of any mindset that holds me back. Because I am a generous giver, God has opened the windows of heaven over my life and is pouring out continuous blessing so I am overflowing with abundance. He has rebuked the devourer for my sake and has released His favor. I have given and it is given to me, good measure,*

176

*pressed down, shaken together and running over. I sow
bountifully, and I reap bountifully. I have everything
I need to do the work of the Lord. I have been made
rich in every way so I can be generous on every occasion so God gets the glory. My God supplies all I need
according to His riches in glory by Christ Jesus. Lord,
send prosperity now. I decree Your word in Jesus' name.*[9]

## Your Declaration
### for Health and Healing

*Death and life are in the power of my tongue so I speak
life over my body. It is God's will for me to be healed.
It is His will that I prosper and live in health even as
my soul prospers. Jesus Christ carried my sickness and
pain on the cross; therefore, I do not need to carry it.
By His stripes I am healed and made whole. The life is
in the blood, and Jesus' shed blood makes me whole.
Jesus lives in me, and His life flows through me. He
came to destroy the works of the devil, which includes
all sickness, disease and pain; therefore, any work of
the devil in my body has already been defeated. I shall
live and not die, and shall declare the works of the Lord.
I command every demonic spirit of sickness, infirmity
or pain to leave my body now by the authority of the
name of Jesus. He is taking all sickness from the midst
of me. The thief comes to steal, kill and destroy, but
Jesus came so I could have abundant life that overflows
with His goodness. The same Spirit who raised Christ
from the dead lives in me and quickens my body to
life. My body is the temple of the Holy Ghost, and all
God's fullness lives in me. I will glorify Him in my body,
which belongs to Him. My healing is springing forth*

*speedily! A merry, joyful, happy heart is good medicine for me. Lord, I will not forget Your benefits of forgiveness, healing and life. Your words impart true life and radiant health into the core of my being. I declare that my body is completely healed now, in Jesus' name and by the power of His word.*[10]

## YOUR DECLARATION
### FOR PEACE

*I live under God's covenant of peace. I keep my mind focused on Him, and He gives me perfect peace in return. I let the peace of God rule over me, and it guards my heart and mind against all negative or destructive thoughts or lies. I will not be anxious, worried or fearful about anything but will be saturated in faith-filled prayer. I guard my heart with all diligence, for out of it flow the issues of life. God who is my inspiration and fountain of hope will fill me with overflowing and uncontainable joy and perfect peace as I put my trust in Him. Then the power of the Holy Spirit will surround my life with His super-abundance until I radiate with hope. God will even cause my enemies to make peace with me. I will make every effort to live at peace with others, and I will turn from evil and will seek peace and pursue it. I bind every spirit of confusion, contention, anxiety, fear, worry, hopelessness and doubt, and command them to leave me and my home in Jesus' name. I cast my cares upon Him for He cares for me. The God of peace is crushing Satan under my feet. I will, therefore, go out with joy and be led forth with peace. When I am weary I come to the Lord and give Him my heavy burden, and He gives me rest. I join my life with His and*

*learn His ways and find refreshment and rest in Him.*
*I will not get weary in doing good, for in due season I*
*will reap if I do not give up. I receive God's promise of*
*peace for myself, my family, my home and all those I*
*love. I decree this in Jesus' name.*[11]

## YOUR DECLARATION
### FOR YOUR FAMILY

One of the greatest hearts' desires of believers is to see our
families living in God's plan and fulfilling His purposes. Some
people have natural family; some have loved ones who are
"family" though not related genetically. Some people have
biological children; some have "spiritual" children who perhaps live in another household. Whatever the dynamic of
your "family," you can make the following decrees over your
home, your children (both natural and spiritual) and those
you love.

*God is my Father and I am His child. My home, there-*
*fore, will reflect the Kingdom of God. I dedicate my*
*family to the Lord so we can know Jesus with all our*
*hearts. My family, children and children's children will*
*be blessed for a thousand generations. Generation after*
*generation will declare more of Your greatness and*
*more of Your glory. My children will serve the Lord and*
*will flourish like the stars of the sky and like the sand*
*on the beaches. They will glorify You and will defeat*
*all their spiritual enemies. The world will be blessed*
*because of them. I will train them in Your ways and*
*when they are adults those values will be with them*
*for life. I honor my mom and dad and bless them, and*
*God will give me a long life. My home will be a place*

*where love abides. My love will be large and incredibly patient. I will be gentle and consistently kind to others. I refuse to be jealous when blessing comes to someone else. I will not brag about my own achievements or inflate my own importance. I will never traffic in shame and disrespect; nor will I selfishly seek my own honor. I will not be easily irritated or quick to take offense. I will joyfully celebrate honesty and hold a standard for right and wrong. My home will be a safe place of shelter, for it never stops believing the best for my family. I will never "take failure as defeat," for I will never give up. I will never stop loving my family—ever! I will never let ugly or hateful words come from my mouth, but instead I will let my words become beautiful gifts that encourage others. I will do this by speaking words of grace to help others. I will lay aside every bitter word, temper tantrum, revenge, profanity and insult. Instead I will be kind and affectionate toward my family. I will live in forgiveness knowing that God has graciously forgiven me. I decree the blessings of the Lord over my family and its generations for today and for each day forward, in Jesus' name.*[12]

## Your Declaration
### for Your Nation

*I decree that because God so loved the world, I will also love the world and will pray for my nation. I pray for my political leaders and representatives on the local, regional and national level, interceding with intense passion so the people in our nation can live tranquil, undisturbed lives as we worship the awe-inspiring*

*God with pure hearts. I know that praying for them— whether I like them or not, whether they are godly or not—is pleasing to the Lord. (Pause and pray for your leaders.) God has given me nations as my inheritance and the uttermost parts of the earth as my possession. My nation will be my legacy. If my nation has strayed from following the Lord, I will humble myself and pray and seek God's face and cry out for my nation to turn from its wicked ways. I know then the Lord will hear my cry and will forgive the sins of my nation and re- store health to my land. (Repent here for any specific sins you can think of for your nation.) I decree what God says, that righteousness exalts a nation and that sin is a reproach to any people. I also declare that the nation whose God is the Lord is blessed. From the four corners of the earth, the peoples of the world will remember and return to the Lord. Every nation will come and worship Him; for the Lord is King of all and takes charge of all the nations. I will seek the peace and prosperity of my city and pray to the Lord for it, knowing that if it prospers, I will prosper. Since the fear of the Lord is the beginning of wisdom and knowledge of the Holy One is understanding, I decree these things for my land. I bind every demonic, antichrist force that is trying to rob my nation and separate it from God's covenant. I decree that the eyes of the people will be opened, and they will find Jesus as their Sav- ior. I decree that the mercy of the Lord will triumph over judgment. I decree that my nation will align itself with God's purposes and will become a sheep nation. I decree revival! I decree a great harvest of souls in my nation. I decree that God's glory will dwell in our land. I decree that God will give what is good to my land, and it will yield its increase. I decree this over my nation in Jesus' name.*[13]

## YOUR ACTIVATION

Do you need joy? Do you need strength? Do you need greater anointing from the Holy Spirit operating in your life? Do you need direction, favor or opportunity? You can write your own decree! Here are some steps to make it simple:

1. Write the subject you are seeking the Lord about at the top of your page.
2. Pray in the Holy Spirit, taking time to listen to the Lord regarding what He says about that subject. Listen for His instructions and convictions as well as His promises.
3. Go to the Word of God. Find seven to ten Scriptures to use to write your decree. Use different translations to inspire you as you write. Feel free to paraphrase. Write the Scripture references at the bottom to remind you these are not just your own good ideas but are the Word of God, which has power to heal, save, deliver and empower.
4. Write the decree in such a way that is easy for you to read it out loud. Include what God has spoken to you prophetically, the Scriptures you have found, as well as anything you sense God would have you take authority over or break the power of.
5. Speak this decree out loud daily. You may find that God expands your thought processes to add to the decree. Speak with boldness and authority knowing that God has invited you to come boldly before His throne

of grace to obtain mercy and find help in your time of need (see Hebrews 4:16).

6. Remember, once you decree a thing, it will be established for you. Expect light to shine on your way (see Job 22:28).

7. Watch for breakthrough and victory!

# Notes

**Introduction**

1. *Merriam Webster*, s.v. "declare," last visited August 17, 2020, https://www.merriam-webster.com/dictionary/declare.
2. *Dictionary.com*, s.v. "decree," last visited August 17, 2020, https://www.dictionary.com/browse/decree.
3. *Dictionary.com*, s.v. "decree," last visited August 17, 2020, https://www.dictionary.com/browse/decree.
4. *Cambridge Dictionary*, s.v. "decree," last visited August 17, 2020, https://dictionary.cambridge.org/dictionary/english/decree.
5. James Strong, *The New Strong's Concise Concordance* (Nashville: Nelson, 1996), G3056.
6. See Matthew 12:13; John 5:8; John 11:43; Luke 8:52; Luke 7:14; Luke 13:12 KJV; Mark 4:39.
7. See Acts 3:6–9.
8. *BibleHub*, s.v. "Acts 3:6," last accessed August 17, 2020, https://biblehub.com/acts/3-6.htm.

**Chapter 1: The Power of Words**

1. Kimberly Holland, "Positive Self Talk," *Healthline*, October 17, 2018, https://www.healthline.com/health/positive-self-talk#benefits-of-self-talk.
2. Erin Wildermuth, "The Science of Words," *Michael Hyatt & Co.*, 2020, https://michaelhyatt.com/the-science-of-words.
3. Caroline Leaf, *Switch on Your Brain*, 2013, http://drleaf.com/products/switch-on-your-brain.

**Chapter 2: The Power of Decrees**

1. Jane Hamon, *The Cyrus Decree* (Santa Rosa Beach, Fla.: Christian International Ministries, 2001).

2. Bruce Whyte and Tomi Ajetunmobi, "Still the 'Sick Man of Europe'?," *Glasgow Centre for Population Health*, November 2012, https://www.gcph.co.uk/publications/391_still_the_sick_man_of_europe.

3. *Wikipedia*, s.v. "Spiritualism," last modified May 29, 2020, https://en.wikipedia.org/wiki/Spiritualism.

## Chapter 3: The Time of the Dynamo

1. *Wikipedia*, s.v. "dynamo," last modified June 25, 2020, https://en.wikipedia.org/wiki/Dynamo.

2. Joseph H. Thayer, *Thayer's Greek-English Lexicon of the New Testament* (Grand Rapids: Baker, 1977), 1411.

3. Bill Hamon, *70 Reasons for Speaking in Tongues* (Shippensburg, Pa.: Destiny Image, 2012), 11, 17.

4. Rick Renner, *Sparkling Gems from the Greek, Volume 1*, Harrison House, 2012, https://itunes.apple.com/WebObjects/MZStore.woa/wa/viewBook?id=595408267.

5. Tim Sheets, *Planting the Heavens* (Shippensburg, Pa.: Destiny Image, 2017), 21–22.

## Chapter 4: Activating the Dynamo Anointing

1. OlympicTalk, "Eliud Kipchoge Runs 1:59 Marathon," *NBC Sports*, October 12, 2019, https://olympics.nbcsports.com/2019/10/12/eliud-kipchoge-marathon-two-hours-ineos-159-challenge/.

2. Robert Bright, "Is There a Difference in 100 Times and 100 Fold?," *Ezine Articles*, November 12, 2008, https://ezinearticles.com/Is-There-a-Difference-in-100-Times-and-100-Fold?&id=1684629.

## Chapter 5: The Breaker Is Here

1. *Dictionary.com*, s.v. "breakthrough." last accessed September 2, 2020, https://www.dictionary.com/browse/breakthroughs.

2. Ibid.

## Chapter 6: Divine Reversals

1. *Vocabulary.com*, s.v. "intercession," last accessed September 3, 2020, https://www.vocabulary.com/dictionary/intercede.

2. *Vocabulary.com*, s.v. "intervene," last accessed September 3, 2020, https://www.vocabulary.com/dictionary/intervene.

3. *charis*, Strong's 5485; *parrhesia*, Strong's 3954; *eleos*, Strong's 1656; *boétheia*, Strong's 996.

4. *Wikipedia*, s.v. "Purim," last accessed September 3, 2020, https://en.wikipedia.org/wiki/Purim.

## Chapter 7: Agreeing with the Voice of God

1. Rick Renner, *Sparkling Gems from the Greek, Volume 2*, Harrison House, 2017, https://itunes.apple.com/WebObjects/MZStore.waa/wa/viewBook?id=1226024186.

2. BIN Staff, "Dead Sea Blooms Floral Wonderland for First Time," *Israel-365News*, February 20, 2020, https://www.israel365news.com/145476/dead -sea-comes-to-life-as-rainfall-creates-rare-floral-landscapes/.

3. Sue Surkes, "Rains Bring Stunning Floral Displays to Parched Dead Sea Area," *The Times of Israel*, February 19, 2020, https://www.timesofisrael.com /rains-bring-stunning-floral-displays-to-parched-dead-sea-area/#gs.f54okr.

4. Michael Bradley, "Smith Wigglesworth On the Power of the Word of God, *Bible Knowledge.com*, December 27, 2018, https://www.bible-know ledge.com/smith-wigglesworth-on-the-word/.

### Chapter 8: The Prophet's Reward

1. Pirkei Avot 5:26.

2. Rabbi Frand, "A Man at 30 Days," *torah.org*, June 7, 2002, https:// torah.org/torah-portion/ravfrand-5757-bamidbar/.

3. Rabbi Dr. Hillel ben David, "The Significance of the Number Thirty," *The Watchman*, blog, https://www.betemunah.org/thirty.html; see also Mishnah, *Avot*, 5:21. The Mishnah is a collection of material embodying the oral tradition of Jewish law.

### Chapter 9: A Quantum Leap Season

1. *Dictionary.com*, s.v. "quantum leap," last accessed September 14, 2020, https://www.dictionary.com/browse/quantum-leap?s=t.

2. *Collins Dictionary*, s.v. "quantum leap," last accessed September 14, 2020, https://www.collinsdictionary.com/us/dictionary/english/quantum -leap.

3. "Quantum Physics: Planck's Constant," Lecture, University of Oregon, http://abyss.uoregon.edu/~js/cosmo/lectures/lec08.html.

4. See Jim Gerrish, "Quantum Physics and Faith," *Word of God Today*, last updated September 1, 2020, http://www.wordofgodtoday.com/quantum -physics-faith/.

5. *Dictionary.com*, s.v. "epidemic," last accessed September 14, 2020, www.dictionary.com/epidemic.

6. Alex Atkinson Jr., "The Story of the Chinese Bamboo Tree," (blog), May 3, 2018, www.alexatkinsonjr.com/2018/05/03/the-story-of-the-chinese -bamboo-tree/.

### Chapter 10: Declarations for Breakthrough

1. See Hebrews 4:12; 2 Timothy 3:16; Psalm 119:105; 133; Isaiah 40:8; Jeremiah 15:16; Psalm 107:20; 119:11; Isaiah 55:11; Romans 15:4.

2. Jane Hamon, *Discernment: The Essential Guide to Hearing the Voice of God* (Minneapolis: Chosen, 2019), 139–140.

3. See 1 John 1:9; Psalm 103:12; Psalm 51:10–12.

4. See 2 Corinthians 5:21; Ephesians 1:4–5; Revelation 17:14; James 4:7; Jude 1:24; Isaiah 54:14, 17; Colossians 1:13; Ephesians 3:16; 1 John 4:4; Luke 2:52.

5. See Ephesians 2:6; 2 Timothy 1:7; Luke 9:1; Joshua 1:3; John 14:12; Romans 8:11; Matthew 10:8; Luke 4:18–19; Mark 16:16–18; Matthew 17:20; Matthew 16:9; Matthew 6:10; Matthew 16:18–19.

6. See 2 Corinthians 2:14; 1 Corinthians 15:57; Psalm 18:35; 18:43 TPT; 149:7–9; 1 John 4:4; Ephesians 4:27; 1 Timothy 6:12; Romans 16:20; Ephesians 6:10; Luke 10:19; 1 Peter 5:8; 2 Corinthians 10:3–4; Ephesians 6:14–16 TPT; Psalm 118:25 TPT.

7. See John 10:27; Psalm 85:8; Acts 2:16–18; Ephesians 1:17–18; Isaiah 30:31; Amos 3:8; Jeremiah 1:10.

8. See Psalm 91:2; Psalm 46:1–3; Psalm 17:8; 2 Thessalonians 3:3; Deuteronomy 31:6; Psalm 86:7; Psalm 91:10–11; Matthew 8:23-27; 1 Thessalonians 5:23; Numbers 22:12; Galatians 6:2; Matthew 5:14–16; Deuteronomy 20:4; John 16:33.

9. See Genesis 12:2; 39:3; Deuteronomy 8:18; 7:13; Joshua 1:8; Genesis 24:40; 2 Chronicles 20:20; Psalm 5:2; 34:10; 66:12; 112:3; Proverbs 3:9–10; 11:25; Isaiah 61:7; Exodus 22:7; Malachi 3:10–12; Luke 6:38; 2 Corinthians 9:6–8; Philippians 4:19; Psalm 118:25.

10. See Proverbs 18:20–21; 3 John 2; 1 Peter 2:24; Isaiah 53:4–5; Leviticus 17:11; Psalm 118:17; Galatians 2:20; 1 John 3:8; Romans 8:19; John 10:10; 1 Corinthians 6:19–20; Ephesians 3:19; Isaiah 58:8; Proverbs 17:22; Psalm 103:2–3; Proverbs 4:22 TPT.

11. See Isaiah 54:10; 26:3; Colossians 3:15; Philippians 4:7; 4:6; Proverbs 4:23; Romans 15:13 TPT; Proverbs 16:7; Romans 12:18; Psalm 34:14; 1 Corinthians 14:33; Romans 16:20; Isaiah 55:12; Matthew 11:28–29 TPT; Galatians 6:9; Psalm 85:8.

12. See Psalm 105:8; 145:4; Genesis 22:17–18 MSG; Proverbs 22:6 TPT; Exodus 20:12; 1 Corinthians 13:4–8 TPT; Ephesians 4:29, 31–32 TPT.

13. See John 3:16; 1 Timothy 2:1–2 TPT; Psalm 2:8 NKJV/TPT; 2 Chronicles 7:14 MSG; Psalm 33:12; 22:27–29 TPT; Jeremiah 29:7; Proverbs 9:10; James 2:13; Psalm 85:4–5, 9, 12.

**Jane Hamon** serves, with her husband, Tom, as senior pastor of Vision Church @ Christian International. In their forty years of ministry together, they have built a thriving local church, ministered in more than 65 nations and helped to lead Christian International Ministries, founded by Dr. Bill Hamon. A clear prophetic voice and eloquent teacher, Jane travels extensively ministering at national and international conferences, consulting with leaders, conducting prophetic workshops and teaching at Bible colleges. She is frequently featured on a variety of Christian television programs. A gifted storyteller, she has sprinkled her books—*Dreams and Visions, The Deborah Company, Discernment, The Cyrus Decree* and *Declarations for Breakthrough*—with rich personal experiences, extensive research and valuable teaching. Jane makes her home in beautiful Santa Rosa Beach, Florida, where she enjoys fulfilling some of her favorite roles in life as wife, mother and now "Mimi" to her growing number of grandchildren.

# More from Jane Hamon

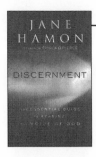

We are called to be Kingdom influencers—to discern the times in which we live, to discern the moving of the Holy Spirit and to discern angels and demons. With extensive expertise and decades of experience, prophetic leader Jane Hamon advises you on how to operate in greater spiritual authority and walk in wisdom as you help build God's Kingdom on earth.

*Discernment*

Does God still speak through dreams and visions today? Absolutely, says Jane Hamon. In this updated edition of her bestselling book, Hamon unravels the scriptural meanings of dreams and visions and offers a 10-step process for interpretation. Learn the language God is using to show you His purposes for your life.

*Dreams and Visions*

# Chosen

 Stay up to date on your favorite books and authors with our free e-newsletters. Sign up today at chosenbooks.com.

 facebook.com/chosenbooks

 @Chosen_Books

 @chosen_books